RYA
Power Schemes
Instructor Handbook

© RYA
First published 2014
Updated April 2015, November 2016
March 2018, February 2019, March
2020, November 2021, November 2022,
December 2023

The Royal Yachting Association
RYA House, Ensign Way,
Hamble, Southampton,
Hampshire SO31 4YA
Tel: 02380 604 100
Web: www.rya.org.uk

We welcome feedback on our publications
at publications@rya.org.uk

You can check content updates for

RYA publications at
www.rya.org.uk/go/bookschangelog

ISBN 978-1-906435974
RYA Order Code G19

Note: While all reasonable care has been taken in the preparation
of this book, the publisher takes no responsibility for the use of the
methods or products or contracts described in this book.

Technical Editor: Laurence West
Cover design: Pete Galvin
Illustrations: Pete Galvin
Photographic credits: Laurence West
Typesetting and design: Velveo Design
Proofreading and indexing: Alan Thatcher
Printed in the UK

Acknowledgements

Rachel Andrews; Pete Galvin; Paul Glatzel, Powerboat Training UK; Anthony Lovell; Ali Selby-Nicholls; Laurence West.

Foreword

If you're reading this book, hopefully it's because you are thinking about training to instruct within the RYA Power schemes, or you are a current Instructor looking to see what this new book brings.

The RYA Power Schemes Instructor Handbook is a valuable reference, full of top tips and background about how people learn. In addition, there is plenty of information on teaching boating in all three schemes.

By combining the three Power schemes of powerboating, personal watercraft and inland waterways, we are able to share good practice across the board, and hopefully inspire good Instructors to take a look at what the other schemes have to offer.

Good luck with your training!

Rachel Andrews
RYA Chief Instructor,
Power

Contents

Part 1

RYA Instructor Code of Conduct for RYA Instructors, Trainers and Examiners   **5**

RYA Equality Policy   **6**

RYA Organisation   **7**

General Considerations   **9**

RYA Instructor Awards   **10**

Techniques for Instructing and Coaching   **11**

Task Structure   **34**

Part 2

The RYA Powerboat Instructor Courses   **35**

The RYA Powerboat Scheme   **43**

RYA Powerboat Level 2 – Powerboat Handling   **44**

RYA Tender Operator Course   **80**

RYA Intermediate Powerboat Day Cruising Course   **90**

RYA Advanced Powerboat Day & Night Course   **94**

Part 3

The RYA Personal Watercraft Scheme   **110**

Part 4

The RYA Inland Waterways Scheme   **127**

Part 5

RYA Powerboat Pre-Instructor Skills Assessment Record   **142**

RYA Power Schemes Instructor Log   **143**

Appendix 1 – Safeguarding and Child Protection   **146**

Appendix 2 – Appeals Procedure   **155**

Appendix 3 – Resources and References   **156**

Appendix 4 – Powerboating and the Environment   **158**

Index   **160**

Part 1

RYA Instructor Code of Conduct for RYA Instructors, Trainers and Examiners

The RYA values and respects the very talented people that make up our training network, and views them as important ambassadors of the RYA's brand and values. This document outlines the code of conduct to which all holders of RYA Instructor qualifications and RYA training appointments (hereafter referred to as Instructors) are required to comply. The code of conduct is intended to make clear to all participants, Instructors and RYA appointment holders the high standards to which all are expected to conform. Instructors must:

- Behave in a manner that is consistent with the values of the RYA, particularly with regards to equality, diversity, inclusivity and sustainability.

- Respect the rights, dignity and worth of every person and treat everyone equally within the context of their boating activity.

- Place the wellbeing and safety of the student above the development of performance or delivery of training.

- Encourage and guide students to accept responsibility for their own behaviour and performance.

- Only develop relationships with students that are appropriate and legal (especially those under 18), whether face to face or in a digital context. Relationships must be consensual, based on mutual trust and respect and must not exert undue influence to obtain personal benefit or reward.

- Ensure the activities they direct or advocate are student focused, and appropriate for the age, maturity, experience and ability of the individual. Always clarify with students (and where appropriate their parents or carers) exactly what is expected of them and what they are entitled to expect.

- Behave appropriately to ensure the safety of Instructors, students and others under your direction.

- Treat all RYA Instructors, appointment holders, staff and other stakeholders with respect.

- Act with integrity in all customer and business to business dealings pertaining to RYA training.

- Read, understand, and comply with the Safeguarding Children and Safeguarding Adults policies and guidelines as detailed on the RYA website at www.rya.org.uk/go/safeguarding.

- Comply with the laws and regulations of the jurisdiction in which they are operating.

- Follow all RYA guidance and standards with regards to specific training or coaching programmes.

- Not do or neglect to do anything which may bring the RYA into disrepute, including through the use of social media.
- Hold relevant, up to date governing body qualifications as approved by the RYA.
- Only teach or provide RYA courses or RYA certification within the framework of an RYA Recognised Training Centre.
- Notify the RYA immediately of any court-imposed sanction that precludes the instructor from contact with specific user groups (for example children or adults at risk) and be aware that certain sanctions may result in the automatic withdrawal of your qualification.
- Notify RYA Training in the event of any health issues that may affect their ability to carry out their responsibilities, including the use of medication which may impact their role.
- Not carry out RYA training, examining or coaching activities whilst under the influence of alcohol or drugs.

Failure to adhere to the RYA Instructor Code of Conduct may result in the suspension or withdrawal of RYA qualifications or appointments. Revised September 2022.

RYA Equality Policy

Objectives

- To ensure boating is accessible and attractive to the widest audience.
- To ensure that the RYA's services, including training schemes, are as accessible as possible, including to people with disabilities.
- To increase the diversity of our Instructors, Coaches and Race Officials.
- To identify and promote more role models at all levels from under-represented groups, including women and girls, people with disabilities, people from BAME backgrounds and LGBT+ people.
- To attract new participants from under-represented groups through targeted initiatives.
- To maintain the Advanced level of the Equality Standard for Sport.

Policy Statement

The Royal Yachting Association is committed to the principle of equality of opportunity and aims to ensure that all present and potential participants, members, Instructors, coaches, competitors, officials, volunteers and employees are treated fairly and on an equal basis, irrespective of sex, age, disability, race, colour, religion or belief, sexual orientation, pregnancy and maternity, marriage and civil partnership, gender reassignment or social status.

Implementation

- The RYA encourages its affiliated clubs and organisations, Recognised Training Centres and other stakeholders to adopt similar policies, so that they offer an experience to participants that is friendly, welcoming and open to all.

- Appointments to voluntary or paid positions with the RYA will be made on the basis of an individual's knowledge, skills and experience and the competences required for the role.
- The RYA will tailor requirements in relation to RYA training schemes which may inhibit the performance of candidates with special needs, provided that the standard, quality and integrity of schemes and assessments are not compromised.
- The RYA will develop further policies for specific subject areas where appropriate (e.g. instructing, race officials).
- The RYA reserves the right to discipline any of its members, qualification holders, appointees, volunteers, or employees who practise any form of discrimination in breach of this policy, in line with the relevant articles, rules, codes of conduct and disciplinary procedures.
- The effectiveness of this policy will be monitored and evaluated on an ongoing basis by the RYA Safeguarding and Equality Manager reporting to the RYA Board and the Sports Council Equality Group.

RYA Organisation

RYA training takes place in Recognised Training Centres (RTCs).

These fall into three main categories:

- Powerboat schools open to the public.
- Sailing clubs that provide courses to their members.
- Restricted organisations such as the Armed Forces and the Police Force.

Recognition is vested in the Principal, who is responsible for all of the training that occurs at the centre, and only they and the Chief Instructor can issue certificates. However, they may not necessarily be qualified to conduct training themselves. If this is so, they will appoint a Chief Instructor (CI) who will fulfil this training role.

Centre recognition is automatically revoked on the change of a Principal, active teaching ceasing or if the centre is sold. Centres risk their recognition being withdrawn if, in the opinion of the RYA, the standards set for recognition are not being maintained.

Gaining Recognition

The starting point to gaining recognition is for the potential Principal to submit an expression of interest form. On receipt of that form we will send further details and access to the full Training Support website so you can see all the information needed to progress. You can find the form at www.cognitoforms.com/RYA2/expressionofinterest.

Once the potential Principal believes they are ready to gain recognition they submit an application form to the RYA along with the relevant fee. The centre will then be visited by an inspector and, provided the inspector's report is satisfactory, recognition will be granted. The school will then be subject to annual or 'spot' inspections administered by the RYA.

Recognition Conditions

During their inspection, the inspector will expect to see the following:

- That the Principal or Chief Instructor holds the relevant and valid RYA Instructor Certificate.
- That the Instructor certificate is supported by a valid and appropriate first aid certificate (see the RYA website www.rya.org.uk for details of accepted certificates).
- That the centre's teaching syllabus and course programmes meet the requirements of the RYA.
- That the facilities are of a satisfactory standard to support the proposed RYA operation.
- That the teaching boat or boats are suitable, appropriate, seaworthy and in good condition.
- That students are using the correct and appropriate personal buoyancy devices for the course on offer.
- That the Principal and/or CI fully understands the RYA requirements necessary for the correct running of an RYA Recognised Training Centre, especially with regard to advertising and the safe running of certificate and non-certificate courses.

The RYA will then classify and recognise the centre based on the inspector's report. It should be noted that RYA Safety Boat and RYA Advanced/Intermediate recognition will only be granted if appropriate boats and qualified staff are available. If there are any doubts as to the suitability of the above, clarification can be given from RYA House prior to an application.

Advertising and use of the RYA Name and Logo

It is only the Principal that may use the RYA name and logo in any advertising material. Instructors (and Examiners) may not do so.

Administration

Once recognition has been granted Principals may open an account with the RYA to bulk purchase certificates and RYA publications to be used on courses. The Principal remains responsible for the correct completion, issuing, registering and recording of certificates at the end of courses and that they are correctly endorsed.

Own-Boat Tuition

RYA-recognised centres may offer own-boat tuition to their customers on the condition that the teaching takes place within the stated operating area of the centre.

The boat used must carry all the usual equipment and safety equipment that would be present on the school's boat(s). Additionally, the owner must ensure that their insurance covers them to receive instruction aboard their own boat.

Own-boat tuition may take place away from a centre, but may only be conducted by an RYA Advanced Powerboat Instructor or an RYA Inland Waterways Instructor.

Centres may not offer 'own-boat' courses only.

General Considerations

Duty of Care

Instructors and trainers must always remember that they are usually teaching relatively inexperienced students who may not be able to make a sound assessment of the risks inherent in the activity. Instructors should not hesitate to make prudent decisions in unfavourable conditions to ensure the safety of the students in their care.

Instructor Health Declaration

I understand that in my capacity as an Instructor I must be able to effectively deliver the relevant syllabus and to look after the safety of my students. Accordingly, I confirm that at all times I can:

1. Communicate effectively with students, other water users and the centre.
2. Recover other craft.
3. Recover a person from the water without assistance.
4. Keep an effective lookout by sight and sound and monitor the safety the vessel and crew.
5. Operate a powerboat independently.

If for any reason, health or otherwise, I believe I may require support to fulfil the requirements above I have provided further details below. I recognise that this information will be used by the RYA to consider what reasonable adjustments may be needed for me to instruct. I recognise that adjustments identified on the training course may be taken into account.

I undertake to:

1. Inform the RYA if my situation in relation to the above requirements changes on a permanent or temporary basis.
2. Submit a health questionnaire to be reviewed by the RYA doctor. In some circumstances a medical assessment may also be required.

Student Health Declaration

In order that they are informed as to any additional risk to students, RYA Recognised Training Centres are strongly advised to include a health declaration in their booking forms. The Principal/Chief Instructor must pass on such information to the individual Instructor responsible for the student.

The declaration should be designed to ensure that the participants are physically and mentally fit to deal with the particular course for which they have applied.

Swimmers

It is recommended that all those participating in powerboat activity should be able to swim. No minimum-level swimming ability is stipulated, but students should be water confident. It is essential that the Instructor in charge of a course knows if any course members are non-swimmers. Non-swimmers may be required to wear lifejackets instead of buoyancy aids.

Carbon Monoxide

All cooking and heating appliances can produce carbon monoxide if not properly ventilated. Exhaust fumes from machinery may also accumulate in enclosed space, and even in open cockpits if stationary or travelling at low speed.

Carbon monoxide is colourless, odourless, and poisoning can be deadly. The first signs are headaches, tiredness, sickness, and dizziness. It is recommended that you fit a carbon monoxide detector and test it regularly.

To ensure adequate ventilation throughout the cabin, make sure that any ventilators are clear of obstructions.

RYA Instructor Awards

Who Teaches Which Courses in the RYA Power Schemes?

Instructors Qualification	Qualified to Teach
RYA Powerboat Instructor	Levels 1 and 2
RYA Powerboat Instructor with Safety Boat	Levels 1 and 2 plus Safety Boat
RYA Advanced Powerboat Instructor*	Levels 1 and 2, Intermediate, Tender Operator and Advanced
RYA Advanced Powerboat Instructor with Safety Boat	Levels 1 and 2, Safety Boat, Intermediate, Tender Operator and Advanced
RYA Powerboat Trainer**	RYA Powerboat Instructor
RYA Powerboat Advanced Trainer	RYA Powerboat Instructor RYA Powerboat Advanced Instructor
RYA Personal Watercraft Instructor	RYA Personal Watercraft Safety RYA Personal Watercraft Proficiency
RYA Personal Watercraft Trainer**	RYA Personal Watercraft Instructor Training
RYA Inland Waterways Instructor*	RYA Inland Waterways Crew RYA Inland Waterways Helmsman's Course
RYA Inland Waterways Trainer**	RYA Inland Waterways Instructor Training

* Only Instructors with qualifications marked * can carry out own-boat tuition when away from training centre base.
** RYA Instructor Training Courses may only be carried out with the knowledge and permission of the RYA Chief Instructor and must have a moderator.
RYA Powerboat and Personal Watercraft courses may only be run at an RYA Recognised Training Centre.
For details of how to become recognised, please contact the RYA Training Department.

Techniques for Instructing and Coaching

Instructing and Coaching Skills

As an RYA Instructor you will deliver teaching material as both an Instructor and 'coach'. Which one it is will depend on a number of factors:

- The type of session (practical or theory).
- The subject (new subject or developing existing techniques and skills).
- The teaching method (discussion, demonstration or student practice).
- The environment (ashore or afloat).
- Number of students.
- Where they are in the RYA scheme.

Your role as an Instructor is to help students learn through teaching them practical and theoretical aspects of the activity. It mostly involves explaining and demonstrating techniques that are new to them.

However, coaching implies a shift towards helping students develop those techniques into skills. It might involve more observation, feedback and questioning to check their understanding of the skills.

A simple, well-used model for this input is shown below. It is by no means the only teaching model, but it has stood the test of time and addresses a number of learning styles that the students will have.

Powerboat Teaching Model – EDICTS

E – Explanation. The Instructor gives a verbal description of the task to be taught. *(Instruction)*

D – Demonstration. The Instructor then demonstrates the skill to be taught. Before handing over the controls, they will check the students' understanding of the task. *(Instruction)*

I – Imitation. The students then attempt to 'copy' the skill that the Instructor has just shown them. *(Coaching)*

C – Correction. The Instructor will give any corrective feedback required to improve student performance. *(Coaching)*

T – Training. Or more correctly, practice. The student can then apply the feedback they have just received. If no feedback was required they can repeat the skill, thereby developing positive reinforcement. *(Coaching)*

S – Summary. Before moving on to the next exercise, the Instructor summarises the skill with the student, the lessons learned and confirms understanding. *(Coaching)*

As can be seen from the model, the RYA Instructor does much more than simply instruct. If they are comfortable and able, after the instructing stage they can use coaching to help their students to develop their own performance.

If you coach your students effectively their performance should improve and any problems that prevent them progressing can be solved.

Effective coaching needs:

- A mutual desire to coach/be coached.
- Good communication between coach and student.
- Empathy towards your students.
- A focus on clear achievable goals.

There are three main processes involved in coaching:

Communication:
Listening; questioning; responding; giving feedback.

Influencing:
Increasing confidence and independence in your students; positively reinforcing things done well.

Helping:
Expressing concern for, and empathy with, their development; establishing support for your students; identifying students' needs and linking this to their goals.

Remember that we are communicating all the time. Our thoughts and emotions can often 'leak' out through our verbal and non-verbal communication.

Instructors and coaches should therefore:

- Develop their verbal and non-verbal communication skills.
- Ensure that they provide positive feedback during sessions.
- Give all students equal or appropriate attention.
- Ensure that they listen to their students, not just talk!

Helping your Students to Learn

The power schemes are fun, practical and exciting activities that require experiential learning – in other words **learning through doing.** It helps to break it down into four stages. In simple terms this means:

- Run a structured activity or session.
- Review and discuss what happened during the session.
- Help your students to learn and be sure about what they know.
- Encourage students to apply their learning to future sessions.

Throughout this process students need:

■ Positive and constructive feedback.

■ Time to reflect.

■ Structured sessions that build on each other.

Exactly how you tackle these four stages can be determined by understanding how your students absorb information and learn new skills.

Absorbing Information

Not everyone sees and experiences the world in the same way. We take in information through our senses:

■ Visual – eyes.

■ Auditory – ears.

■ Kinaesthetic – touch, feel and movement.

These senses are pathways to our brains. None of us uses one pathway exclusively – there is significant overlap between them, but your students are likely to have a preference:

Visual learners

They like:

■ Written information.

■ Pictures and observation.

■ Sessions that have a lot of content to observe, i.e. demonstrations and visual aids.

Auditory learners

They like:

■ Information contained in the spoken word.

■ Clear verbal explanations/ briefings.

■ Verbal feedback.

■ Discussions.

Kinaesthetic learners

They like:

■ Learning through touch and movement.

■ To 'have a go' and see what happens.

By adapting your teaching style to suit these three preferences you should be able to create a learning environment with something for everyone.

Once we have absorbed information, we need to process it in order for us to learn. In the same way that we have a preference for absorbing information, we also tend to have a preference for how we learn from this information. Just as people have a tendency towards left or right-handedness, which influences how they tackle manual tasks, many people have a particular learning style that influences how they approach mental tasks.

As Instructors or coaches, by being aware of different learning preferences or styles we are able to modify our own teaching style to suit that of our students.

Tips for Reinforcing Learning

- Always put new techniques into context – understanding is helped if you see the 'big picture'.

- The average person can deal with approximately seven chunks of information – don't overload them.

- People remember the beginning and end, but often miss the middle – keep demonstrations and explanations short and structured.

- Keep information memorable – use unusual, funny or unexpected ways to illustrate your teaching.

- Use a range of methods to teach important skills in order to cater for your students' range of learning styles – i.e. explaining, showing video footage, visualising, reading, looking at pictures etc.

- Ensure that new skills become well-established with plenty of practice and reinforcement.

- Focus your students on what they should do, rather than what they should not do, or they might end up doing the very opposite to what they should!

Demonstrations are particularly important and useful, so demonstrate whenever possible. People will need time to identify what is being taught, so link the parts into a smooth skill that becomes automatic.

This leads to the 'whole-part-whole' demonstration method, where the skill is executed at normal speed, then broken into detailed parts, then redone at normal speed. In this way both a mental picture and a detailed understanding can be conveyed. This method can be used if the skill is deemed to be too complicated in the first instance.

Top Tips

- What I hear, I forget. What I see, I remember. What I do, I understand.
- Position the students where they can see clearly but are safe. Be aware of any distractions.
- What you do is more important than what you say. Use few words and demonstrate smoothly at normal speed before breaking the manoeuvre down, if required.
- Most instructors talk too much as they demonstrate.

The Four Stages of Learning – Unconscious Incompetence to Unconscious Competence

You can expect your students largely to follow the same stages when learning any new technique. Indeed, as they progress up through the stages with one technique they may begin again at the bottom with new techniques or skills.

Four Stages of Competence

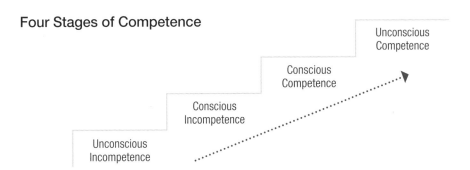

Unconscious Incompetence

Students don't know what they don't know.

Conscious Incompetence

Students are aware of what they don't know. For some this adds clarity, others find it daunting and frustrating.

Conscious Competence

Students are becoming competent but still have to think about what they are doing and how they do it. Following simple sequences will be useful at this stage.

Unconscious Competence

Students now do things with very little conscious thought. Things flow and are effortless.

Basic Skills Model

Instructors should adapt their approach as students develop competence and become more skilful, initially instructing and being directive in their approach to the development of good technique but eventually becoming less directive and more supportive as technique becomes more skilful and adopting a more coaching role.

How and Why People Learn

The Way Students Learn

- Once given a task, they will get on with it. Sometimes it can be difficult to get them to stop.
- They may have difficulty with the goal-orientated and structured approach to learning. They have become used to being lectured. They can find the relaxed RYA session uncomfortable.
- Often they will need to know why they are learning something.
- Encourage them to answer questions and to question the content of the session in general. Don't allow anyone to opt out.
- Ensure that the purpose as well as the aim of the session is made clear at the start.
- Accumulated life experience can be applied to the learning process for good and bad. They may also be used to 'problem solving'. Use this to your advantage and incorporate it into sessions. It may make sessions longer, however.
- They can be reluctant to get things wrong and appear foolish, especially in front of the others, and become frustrated when they do! Reward correct answers/solutions and encourage those who answer incorrectly to find the right ones.

People often learn best through fun and enjoyment. Make your sessions fun and stimulating for all.

What Might Motivate our Students to Learn?

- Making or maintaining social relationships.
- A desire to achieve awards and qualifications.
- Escape or stimulation from everyday life.
- Interest in the subject.
- Lifestyle aspiration.
- Fear of failure.

Being aware of your students' possible motivations for taking the course helps you to shape it, the materials you use and how you structure the groups in which they are placed for teaching.

Barriers to Learning

- Other responsibilities (families, careers, social commitments).
- Lack of time.
- Environment – being wet and cold!
- Feelings – looking or feeling silly.
- Scheduling problems – when courses take place.
- Insufficient confidence.
- Inappropriate teaching methods.
- Culture clash – young Instructor vs. middle-aged student.
- Personality clashes – between student and Instructor.
- Having to learn, if told by partner or spouse but not interested or ready.
- Fear of failure (again).

Fear

Fear is one of the main barriers which you, a good Instructor, can help the students overcome.

Students normally have three principal fears when trying something for the first time:

Fear of failure – Be clear about their progress throughout the course. Encourage them to try things out, even if it means making mistakes. If the course is assessed, let your students know the outcome.

Fear of the unknown – Keep your students fully informed throughout the course, the stages they will go through and why you are structuring the course that way.

Fear of not being liked or fitting in – Break the ice early and encourage students to work together and get to know each other.

When learning boating, the students are often given charge of a large, powerful and expensive craft. It is little wonder that they can sometimes feel intimidated by this. When this is linked to the other barriers to learning mentioned previously, then the Instructor shouldn't be surprised if students don't pick up the skills that they are being taught immediately. Instructors can help by carefully choosing the skills to be learned, the pace at which they are delivered, the area chosen to introduce them and which student is at the controls when the skill is first attempted.

People Skills for Instructors

What your Students Think of You

How you are perceived by others determines your credibility and therefore the influence you will have over them. First impressions are vital as it is estimated that up to 90 per cent of people's opinions of you are formed in the first four minutes of meeting you. Therefore, you will start with a disadvantage if your students arrive for the course only to find you stressed and bedraggled, trying to open up the centre, tidy up the mess left by the previous group, getting equipment stores open and boats afloat.

Tips for gaining your students' trust:

■ The first four minutes of any encounter are the most important and set the scene.

■ Always set up early and be ready for their arrival.

■ Pay attention to your personal appearance and grooming as this can exert an inordinate influence on their first impression of you.

■ Listen to your students and respect what they tell you – the more you listen, the more you can influence them.

■ Spend time with them to enable a rapport to develop.

What You Need to Know about your Students

Remember that amongst your students you are going to have widely differing ages, genders, backgrounds, skills, hopes, fears, expectations and aspirations.

It's a good idea to gather as much information as possible on these areas from your students prior to the course. Some of this can be done on booking forms or simple questionnaires. Questions you might want to ask of beginners:

■ Why do you want to learn to drive a boat?

■ Have you done any boating before, when, where etc.?

■ Do you take part in any other water sports?

■ What will you do once you have gained your award?

…and so on.

Being prepared with this information can help you to:

■ Create the right environment.

■ Be warm, welcoming and friendly.

■ Tell them a bit about yourself.

■ Get them all talking about themselves.

■ Tell them what to expect (and what not to expect).

■ 'Create the course' (together).

■ Break the ice.

Communication Skills

Communication is more than just words. We are constantly communicating, even when we are saying nothing.

Research has shown that 55 per cent of your communication is determined by your body language, posture and eye contact, 38 per cent by your tone of voice, and only seven per cent by your actual words. Therefore, to get your message across, concentrate on how you talk, not just what you say. Whatever you say, typically your students will:

- Filter: Pick out more or less important bits for themselves.
- Distort: Interpret things for themselves.
- Delete: Remove any bits that they find unclear or too difficult.

Remember that often **less is more** – keep your messages simple and free of jargon, and back them up with demonstrations and practical examples.

Check your students' understanding of new information as often as possible, using open questions to enable them to confirm what you have said or what you want them to do.

Remember – the worst question in the world is 'Do you understand?' There will only ever be one answer – 'yes'.

Non-verbal Messages

People use a variety of behaviour to maintain a smooth flow of communication, such as head-nods, smiles, frowns, laughter etc. Your students' facial expressions provide you with some feedback on the session.

Glazed or down-turned eyes indicate boredom or disinterest, as does fidgeting. Fully raised eyebrows signal disbelief and half raised indicate puzzlement. The posture of the group enables you to judge their attitude and mood.

Communication Blocks

Communication difficulties between the Instructor and the student can happen for a number of reasons:

- The student's perception of something is not the same as yours.
- The student may jump to a conclusion instead of working through the process of hearing, understanding and accepting.
- The student may lack the knowledge and understanding of what you are trying to teach.
- The student may lack the motivation.
- The Instructor may have difficulty in expressing what they want to say.
- Emotions may interfere in the communication process.
- There may be a clash of personalities.

Effective Communication

Effective communication contains six elements:

- **CLEAR** Ensure that the information is presented clearly.
- **CONCISE** Be concise. Do not lose the message by being long-winded.
- **CORRECT** Be accurate. Avoid giving misleading information.
- **COMPLETE** Give all the information and not just part of it.
- **COURTEOUS** Be polite and non-threatening. Avoid conflict.
- **CONSTRUCTIVE** Be positive. Avoid being critical and negative.

Always check that:

- You have your students' attention.
- Your students are accepting what you are saying.
- You are giving clear explanations and demonstrations.
- Your students have understood.

Always consider:

- WHY you need to communicate.
- WHO you are communicating with.
- WHERE and WHEN the message will best be delivered.
- WHAT you will be explaining or demonstrating.
- HOW you will get the information across.

Communication while afloat is particularly important but often goes wrong, so remember:

- Keep verbal communication to a minimum.
- Project your voice towards your students – it can get lost in the wind.
- Never shout – it implies that you are angry.
- Position your students or yourself where they can hear you best, but remember the 'instructor' position.
- Regularly confirm understanding.

Presentation Skills

It is normal for inexperienced Instructors to be nervous about giving presentations, despite the fact that they know their subject matter well but, with the right frame of mind and a bit of practice, the nerves will soon start to disappear.

The fear often revolves around things going wrong, such as:

- I'll dry up.
- No one will be interested.
- I'll be boring.
- They won't like me.
- I don't know enough about my subject.
- They'll ask me difficult questions.
- I'll make a fool of myself.

However, being aware of these fears can help you to ensure that they don't come true.

Good Presentations Depend on Several Elements:

The Content

Write down what you know about the subject onto a large sheet of paper in the form of headings. If you can, try to group related things together. Even subjects that may not initially seem relevant to the presentation may help identify other things that are. Keeping your objectives in mind, sort out the relevant material using the 'must know, should know, could know' formula. Keep only the 'must know' and discard the rest for now.

Group the 'must knows' under three structured headings – a) introduction, b) main body, and c) summary and close.

- Consider the time available for the presentation. After all the 'must knows' have been included, can any of the others be added in? If so, choose the most relevant first.
- Group the points you have decided to include under subject headings but do not consider the sequence at this stage.
- Place the subject headings in a logical, interesting order.
- Put a time allocation on each subject and the use of each visual aid.
- Make working notes for the presentation.

The Words

- Clear, concise, jargon-free language.
- Think before you speak – don't 'think out loud'!
- Emphasise the important bits.
- Summarise what you've said and ask questions.

How you Say them

- Vary your voice tone and pitch.
- Vary the pace.
- Speak in a conversational way.
- If you speak quickly, build in pauses.
- Project your voice.
- Use silences – pause before important points.
- Don't fade at the end of sentences.

How you Look while Saying them

- Good posture – stand tall, shoulders back.
- Make eye contact with all of the audience.
- Standing or sitting – decide which is best for you.
- Keep your head up.
- Avoid distracting mannerisms – get a friend to tell you if you have any.
- Dress to help your credibility – you can be smart and casual!
- Stop to breathe, look, listen, speak.

Structuring Presentations – Beginning, Middle and End

- Do not start talking until you are fully in position and ready.
- An early smile helps to relax both you and them.
- Rehearse your presentation, and modify as necessary.
- Have a plan 'B'.

The Beginning

Prepare an introduction that will attract your audience's attention. Tell them:

- Whether you will be giving them a handout or letting them know they should make their own notes, what you plan to cover and your structure (give headings).
- How long you will take.
- When they can ask questions.

If you are nervous, know your first few sentences off by heart and never apologise for your knowledge or speaking ability. Be relaxed and conversational.

Some possible ways of opening are:

- Ask a question that requires a show of hands.
- Begin with a quotation or tell a story.
- Ask the audience to do something.
- Describe a true (or imaginary) situation.
- State a significant and challenging statistic.
- Challenge the audience.
- Tell a joke (but only if you are really good at this).

The opening few moments of a presentation are very important. You want the audience to sit up and think 'this is going to be stimulating and important'.

The Middle

After you have grabbed your audience's attention with your introduction, move on to the bulk of your presentation, 'the middle'.

Remember that attention wanders and your audience will pay most attention at the beginning and end of sections, so keep them short with clear headings and summaries.

The End

- Summarise your key points.
- Emphasise your themes.
- Make it significant.
- Do not end with something like 'that's about all I have to say so I'll end now'.
- Always stop before your audience want you to.
- Link back to your opening. For instance, 'When I started I said I would…'. And perhaps go through a check list of points in your intro.

Some ways of ending are:

- Issue a challenge (a gentle one).
- Raise a laugh and tell a final anecdote.
- Relate to a future point.
- Finish with a quotation.
- Ask questions about what you've said.
- Give a quiz.

Be aware of, but not too self-conscious of, your body movements:	
Posture	Sit or stand up straight – but not rigid.
Hands	Don't be afraid of using them – as long as they are not distracting the audience.
Movement	It is fine to move about as long as, once more, this does not become a distraction.
Position	Avoid obstructions to the audience's view of you.
View of your visual aids	Never turn your back on the audience – they won't hear you.
Eyes	Maintain eye contact with the whole audience.
Notes	Do not talk to your notes or visual aids.

Handling Questions

Set the Rules for Questions

Set rules for questions in the beginning, i.e. save questions for the end or ask questions whenever you like (which might be more common and useful in an informal environment). Remember, you are the leader, so lead. Whichever rule you set, make sure it's followed. Reserve the right to stop taking questions in order to ensure you have sufficient time to cover all subjects.

What to Say when you Don't Know the Answer

Honesty is the only policy when presenting to a group, but blatantly admitting 'I don't know' in response to a direct question may be disastrous. No one can know the answer to every question, but it's how the situation is handled that separates great presenters from amateurs. Don't get lulled into thinking you have seen and heard it all on a particular topic. At any time someone can come out of left field with a question you have never thought of before.

The following strategies can help you field even the toughest questions with confidence.

Reflection

Repeat the question and toss it back to your audience. 'Does anyone here have any experience with that?' The audience can save you without ever realising it. In fact, they will love to be involved and share their knowledge. After you have fielded their contributions, summarise and add your own ideas.

'I don't know the answer to that but I will find out for you.'

This is an old standard and it works well. It is an opportunity to go the extra mile, expand your knowledge, and impress your audience.

Defer to the Expert

This is a more sophisticated version of the 'Reflection' technique. Sometimes a question is legitimately outside of your area of expertise but there may be someone more experienced within the school or centre that you can pass it on to. You will need to decide who presents the answer – you or them.

Compliment the Questioner

For this to be effective, the compliment must be sincere. For example, 'That's a good question. I've never thought about it that way. Does anyone here have any ideas on that?' You might also combine this technique with 'I'll get back to you.'

Use of Visual Aids

Skilful use of visual aids can greatly enhance your presentation, but don't let them take over. Always remember that your relationship with your audience is key and visual aids are just there to support you. They can take the attention off you periodically and allow you to think ahead.

Some general tips:

- The best visual aid is a live example of your subject matter, i.e. a buoyancy aid, a safety pack, an anchor, etc. Use it as often as you can.
- If the visual aid is too comprehensive, your audience will switch off from you and read the visual aid instead.
- Whenever possible use pictures, diagrams, graphs and colour rather than lots of writing.
- Do not use too many different visual aids as you can end up in a terrible muddle.

White Boards/Blackboards

- The most common form of visual aid.
- Avoid light-coloured pens as they are difficult to see at the back of the room.
- Make sure your pens have ink in them!
- Practise writing in large letters.
- Practise drawing diagrams.
- Why not use a mobile camera phone to capture the details before rubbing it off, then emailing it to the students if necessary?

Flip Charts

- Work well for interaction.
- Can be prepared in advance.
- Test your pens on the back of a sheet beforehand.
- Write a note for yourself in faint pencil (the audience won't see it).
- Attach key sheets to the wall if appropriate.
- Pre-draw any diagrams in faint pencil. Then, when the time comes, overdraw them with a marker pen.

Data Projectors

- PowerPoint: good for large, formal presentations.
- Useful for key words, images and video.
- Professional effect.
- Easy to update.
- Practise well beforehand.
- Avoid too many effects and sounds!

DVDs

- Must be relevant and up to date.
- Use of video cameras for filming your students and playing footage of their own performance can be very powerful.
- Do not dwell on students' mistakes, no matter how funny.
- Use very sparingly.

Models (very useful for IRPCS)

- Useful for highlighting specific topics.
- Easy to carry and set up.
- Students can get involved easily.
- Usually very 'low tech'.

The 'Real Thing'

- Better than just about anything else.
- Illustrates the point perfectly.
- Students can get 'hands on'.
- Saves making diagrams, drawings etc.

Whichever method you use, avoid:

- Too many words.
- Too much detail.
- Overcrowded slides.

- Bland images.
- Talking to the visual aid.
- Leaving the visual aid on display when you have finished with the subject matter.

Making your Visual Aids Accessible

Every individual has a different perception of what they see and read. The shape and size of words can appear different to each reader. This is especially true when working with students that may have dyslexia. Consider that 10 per cent of your clients may be dyslexic. Remember that changes you make to accommodate dyslexic people are good practice for everyone.

Adopting some simple strategies can help everyone to get the most from reading written information.

Font Style

- Fonts should be rounded with space between letters and reflect ordinary writing. Fonts such as Arial or Comic Sans are good.
- Where possible, use lower-case letters rather than capitals. Using capital letters for emphasis can make text harder to read.

Paper

- Avoid light text on a dark background.
- Use coloured paper instead of white. Cream or off-white provides a good alternative.
- Matt paper is preferable to glossy paper, as this reduces glare.
- Ensure the paper is heavy enough to prevent text showing through from the back.

Presentation Style

- Limit lines to 60 to 70 characters to avoid putting strain on the eyes.
- Use short paragraphs with space between each line and paragraph.
- Use wide margins and headings.
- Use boxes for emphasising important text.
- Use bold to highlight words rather than italics or underlining.
- Keep lines left justified with a ragged right edge.
- Use bulleted or numbered lists.
- Use this page as a guide.

Writing Style

- Write in short, simple sentences.
- Be conscious of where sentences begin on the page. Starting a new sentence at the end of a line makes it harder to follow.
- Try to call the readers 'you': imagine they are sitting opposite you and you are talking to them directly.
- Give instructions clearly. Avoid long explanations.
- Stop and think before you start writing so you are clear about what you want to say.
- Use short words where possible.
- Keep your sentences to an average of 15 to 20 words.
- Be concise.

Using Flip Charts

- Keep essential information grouped together.
- Print lower case rather than using joined writing.
- Write large. It's easier for you and easier to read.
- Flow charts or models are ideal for explaining procedures.
- Use pictures and diagrams.
- List 'dos' and 'don'ts' rather than continuous text.
- Use small chunks of information, and plenty of white space, to improve readability.
- Use plain, simple and jargon-free language.
- Avoid red, orange or green as they can be hard to read for some people such as those with dyslexia.

Briefing and Debriefing

RYA Instructors are fortunate in that they can instantly begin teaching their students as soon as they move to the teaching boat. Using a structured approach to deliver the information needed to achieve each task will help both the Instructor and student.

Brief

This should occur before every on-water session and before every new skill is introduced. Be careful though, because if it's too long the students will switch off, becoming disinterested and perhaps missing a vital piece of information that may have a bearing on their performance or safety.

The briefing should include:

- The task – what the students should be doing.
- How to achieve the task with an explanation and demonstration if required.
- The duration of the task.
- The teaching area including the boundaries, how they will be marked and any hazards to be aware of.
- How and where feedback will take place.
- What the students should do in an emergency if the Instructor is incapacitated (this should only need to be given in the initial safety brief).

Once this has been given, it's only of real use if it's been understood by the students. Don't fall into the trap of checking understanding by asking the classic wrong question of 'Does everyone understand?', because there will only ever be one answer – 'yes!' Instead, ask questions that relate directly to the information that's just been given, such as 'What technique or task are we going to perform?', 'How will it be performed?', 'Where will it be carried out?', 'What will the crew do?' If the correct answers are coming back, then it's likely that an efficient brief has been given. The classic 'give away' sign is when you start the task the students ask themselves 'What do we do, what did the instructor say?'

The Task

The task must be chosen to suit the ability of the student. Part of the skill of instructing is to assess the student's ability and provide tuition at a challenging but not impossible level. It is very frustrating for someone with a natural flair or with some experience to be taught at the pace of the slowest beginner.

Once the task has been set, allow the student to feel responsible for it. Do not continually interrupt – if you have briefed well it should be unnecessary. If events start to go wrong, a quiet word will allow the student to correct the mistake while still being in control. Never elbow students out of the way to demonstrate your skill: the idea is that they demonstrate theirs.

Occasionally, if you can, allow a mistake to be made to illustrate a point, but only do this if you feel it does not compromise safety, will not damage the boat and it is a good learning opportunity.

Debrief

Good instructing and coaching allows for students to learn in a variety of ways and is one important element of the Instructor's repertoire, but providing good feedback during a debrief will always help the student understand more and maximise that learning. Indeed, giving effective feedback is often said to be the one skill that separates the average Instructor from the very good Instructor.

To be most efficient, feedback should happen as soon after the event as possible. This implies that it should happen on the water as the student is performing the skill, or just afterwards. If this is possible, then that's where it should happen. It needs to be more sophisticated than a

'Well done, that was great, how does everyone feel?' Each student ought to be provided with information on what they have achieved, what went well, what didn't go so well and how to put right areas that need improvement.

Any feedback methods will need some common elements to be in place beforehand. They are:

- Be clear what the task is and know how to perform it.
- Ensure that it is achievable by the students.
- Observe the session/skill carefully.
- Record what has taken place with either a good memory or notes, if necessary.
- The Instructor always remains in charge of the session, and hence safety, throughout.

Two popular feedback models being used are 'hamburger' or 'traffic light'.

The 'Hamburger', 'Sandwich' or 'Layer Cake'

It's tried and tested but has been around for a long time now. Also, the students eventually recognise the pattern.

The top
Give praise for aspects that have gone well. Be specific. ▶

The filling
What's not gone well and how to correct it. Be specific and use the 'rule of 3', i.e. three key things that at this stage will lead to improvement. ▶

The bottom
More praise, finishing on a positive note. ▶

The 'Traffic Light'

It's along similar lines, but opens up more opportunity for a flowing discussion. This works with most students, but there are some out there who prefer a more direct approach and just want to be told what's going wrong and how they can put it right!

If a student invites this as a coaching solution from the Instructor there's no harm in accepting the invitation, providing it's done with a degree of sensitivity.

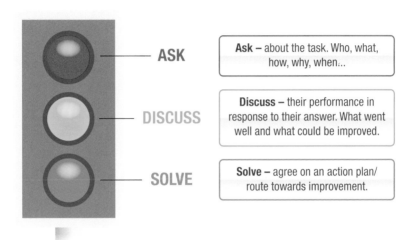

ASK — Ask – about the task. Who, what, how, why, when...

DISCUSS — Discuss – their performance in response to their answer. What went well and what could be improved.

SOLVE — Solve – agree on an action plan/ route towards improvement.

1. Ask the student about aspects of their performance. Start with open and general questions, then focus in on specific areas.

2. Discuss these areas using the response to the questions given by the student.

3. Solve any problems firstly by encouraging the student to seek the solution. If they can't, the Instructor will do this for them. However, the student should always be the one who identifies the problem and then provides the solution with guidance and help from the Instructor.

By allowing the student to start analysing their performance of the skills being taught, then seeking ways of improving their performance, the student will learn how to continue this process after they have left the environment of the structured session led by an Instructor.

In effect, the Instructor is preparing the student for when the Instructor is no longer there. After this training, the student should be able to continue with their own progress using the skills and learning process delivered by the Instructor.

Assessing your Students' Abilities

There is an element of assessment in every RYA training course, not just the formal assessment that leads to the award of a certificate but also the more informal assessment that takes place throughout the course, no matter how short or long it may be. Assessment is about understanding how the student is performing against a set of standards or expectations.

This might be summarised in three stages:

■ Initial assessment.

■ Formative assessment.

■ Summative assessment.

For example, when an Instructor or coach first meets their students an 'initial assessment' takes place where the Instructor tries to establish what experience and skills the students already have. This initial assessment may be a simple discussion of previous powerboating experience, or it may be made slightly more formal by asking students to set out on paper what they have done previously. The first on-water session is also used to establish the starting point for the course. The benefit of this approach is to enable the Instructor to structure the course and the content to suit the students' actual levels of ability rather than their assumed level. There may also be formal checks to be made on pre-course requirements for Instructor training.

As the course progresses the Instructor will be carefully monitoring students' progress to see if the pace is too fast, too slow or just right to be challenging, informative and achievable. This can be described as the 'formative assessment' and once again could be either formal or informal. Group discussions, quizzes and one-to-one discussions may be useful here.

Finally, at the end of the course the Instructor or coach has to decide, with the help of the Chief Instructor, whether or not the objectives of the training have been achieved. This is the 'summative assessment' and once again could use a range of methods to achieve an objective view of the assessment criteria. However, it will be based almost entirely on whether the student 'can' perform a skill successfully without input or not. Ultimately the question will be whether to award the certificate. To help you in this the following statements or measures may be of use, but never forget that most people are doing this for fun, and recognising the progress that your students have made by the award of certificates is more likely to motivate them to continue than withholding the certificate because they cannot perform the task every time!

Certificates

RYA certificates provide a great incentive to continue training, providing a clear measure of an individual's progress. However, they can become a discouragement to the weak student as the prospect of gaining a certificate fades. The Chief Instructor will advise on the importance of keeping everyone informed of their progress through the course, and what they can realistically achieve. This could involve breaking the news that an RYA certificate is not possible by the end of the course. The Instructor should explain what can be achieved and agree with the student how to get the best possible value out of the course.

From then on, the Instructor should set goals, point out strengths and weaknesses and offer encouragement. They should point out how much has been achieved as the course progresses so that by the final debrief both can be satisfied that the course was worthwhile.

If students are not kept informed tension will build up, with students discussing among themselves whether they are passing or failing. During the final debrief, Instructor teaching may be blamed for lack of results. This lack of communication between Instructor and student is one of the most common reasons for complaints about RYA courses. Remember that many of the people taught are highly successful and respected in their own field. The only skill the Instructor may have that they haven't is the ability to drive a powerboat and be able to teach others the skills required. Ensure they retain their dignity and a positive attitude towards their Instructor and the activity. This is one of the most skilful aspects of instructing.

Task Structure

In a previous section, the EDICTS teaching method was the focus. This model was for the benefit of the Instructor teaching the session. However, it would be useful if the student had their own model to use while they were learning, as this would give them a structure for each and any task that they would subsequently attempt.

A useful model for the student is PAME.

P – Planning. Whatever task or skill is being attempted, the student should plan what they are about to do before the boat is moved. This will include taking into account the wind, the tide/current, other water users, boat preparation, crew briefing, any obstructions/hazards (and their escape plan).

A – Approach. After the planning stage, it should then become clear how fast and from which direction the approach should be. Any boat preparation not already done can be carried out now, along with allocation of tasks to the crew. All the points addressed during the planning stage still need to be paid attention to during the approach.

M – Manoeuvre. This is the 'task' itself, i.e. coming alongside, turning in a confined space etc. Although it will require attention, the other factors from above should not be ignored.

E – Escape (already addressed at the planning stage). Whatever the task, the students should be able to extricate themselves from it, i.e. in coming alongside, if they are not happy with any element of the approach stage they should be able to safely 'abort' the exercise and take themselves into a safe space in order to reassess before making another attempt. Using the 'escape' plan should not be considered as a failure. It should be viewed instead as 'good seamanship'.

The different content of the power schemes courses requires the Instructor to deliver information at varying levels. Some content needs only a brief explanation and guidance given as to where more information can be found. Other subjects require much more input and the students need to be able to show their Instructor that they have a sound grasp of what has been taught by being able to physically perform the task themselves, with no further input from the Instructor.

These different levels will be referred to often and can be summarised as follows:

Knowledge of the subject – the subject will be briefly explained. There will be familiarisation on the course and information provided on where to find out more.

Understands the subject – the subject will be covered in greater depth. Students will be asked to demonstrate a basic understanding and leave the course able to develop their own skill in this area further. Confirmation of understanding of the subject may be asked for in a variety of ways on the course.

Can demonstrate a level of proficiency in the subject – the subject will be covered in great depth, including background theory. The Instructor will give practical demonstrations that the students will repeat until they are able to demonstrate good skills in this subject.

Part 2

The RYA Powerboat Instructor Courses

The RYA Powerboat Instructor Course

Courses are run at a number of centres and clubs around the world. Each course will be run by an appointed RYA Powerboat Trainer who has been trained and assessed to deliver the course to the required standard. Each course will be moderated on the last day by another, separate RYA Powerboat Trainer, who will assist the course trainer in reaching a decision on the performance of the candidate(s).

The course is preceded by a **skills assessment** to ensure that candidates have the powerboat driving skills required of an Instructor. These skills are based on RYA Powerboat Level 2 skills. Candidates considering enrolling on an RYA Powerboat Instructor course should ensure that they possess driving skills to the required standard. The assessment will be carried out by an RYA Powerboat Trainer at a Recognised Training Centre or affiliated club.

Duration:	Minimum four hours
Carried out at:	Powerboat Recognised Training Centres or affiliated club
Assessed by:	RYA Powerboat Trainer
Eligibility:	RYA Powerboat Level 2
Minimum age:	16 years
Ratio:	Maximum 1:6, using two boats

How to become an RYA Powerboat Instructor

Course prerequisites:

- Hold the RYA National Powerboat Certificate Level 2.
- Hold a valid first aid certificate (RYA-approved – go to www.rya.org.uk for further details).
- Possess at least five years' experience of practical powerboating in a variety of types of boats. For those who are powerboating full-time, this may be reduced to one season.
- Be a minimum age of 16 years old. No candidates under this age will be accepted onto a training course.
- Before being accepted onto a training course, candidates must enrol onto and successfully pass the RYA Powerboat Instructor skills assessment.
- Candidates wishing to be able to teach the RYA Safety Boat course must firstly hold the award themselves.

Although not mandatory, it is strongly recommended that potential candidates attend and 'shadow' an RYA Powerboat Level 2 course before committing to the Instructor course. This will give an indication of what will be expected of candidates during the Instructor course.

Candidates for the pre-entry assessment will be expected to demonstrate competence in the following manoeuvres:

- Hold off a mark.
- Pick up and secure to a buoy.
- Moor alongside up/downtide.
- Turn using warps.
- Turn in a confined space.
- Recover a man overboard (dummy).
- Stop/start engine.
- Planing speed runs including 'Figure 8' and 'U' turns.

Syllabus

The RYA Powerboat Instructor course is conducted over three days and will contain the following elements:

- The theory of teaching – principles of practical instruction.
- Delivering theory subjects.
- Preparation and effective use of visual aids.
- Lesson & programme planning.
- Teaching styles.
- Practical driving.
- Reviewing & feedback skills.
- The standards required by the RYA.
- Assessing student ability.
- Structure of the RYA National Powerboat scheme.
- Developing student skills along a progressive pathway.
- The requirements for running an effective RYA Powerboat school, including conditions for recognition.

During the course the candidate will receive input from the trainer and also from the other candidates. They will be asked to show the following:

- Knowledge of the subject of powerboating.
- Ability to deliver effective teaching sessions.
- Ability to demonstrate all elements of the RYA Powerboat Level 2 syllabus.
- Ability to deliver at least one theory session ashore.
- Be able to demonstrate safety awareness for themselves and students throughout.

Candidates will be asked to teach three distinct groups on the course:

- Each other, i.e. the other candidates on the course.
- The course trainer/moderator.
- Real students or 'guinea pigs' who have been asked to attend to assist the course. These must not be paying students on a recognised course.

Course Moderation

The course will be moderated by an external moderator (an RYA Powerboat Trainer) who has not been associated with the course. They will view the candidates and help decide on the overall course outcome. They will also review the course in general to ensure that it has adhered to the standards set by the RYA.

The moderator (and trainer) will be looking for the following:

- Effective teaching of practical aspects of the RYA Powerboat Level 2 syllabus, preferably with 'real' students.
- Effective delivery of a theory topic ashore.
- Delivery of an unprepared short presentation on any aspect of the syllabus.
- Demonstration of an understanding and ability to deliver the basic navigation required for a pilotage plan.
- Demonstration of an awareness and application of safety aspects required for powerboating for all participants.

Successful candidates will be issued with an RYA Instructor certificate, which will be valid for five years if supported by an approved valid first aid certificate.

The Instructor certificate will remain valid if the following criteria are met:

- It is no more than five years since it was issued.
- The holder also holds a valid first aid certificate approved by the RYA. See RYA website for details.
- Certificates may be revalidated by obtaining and returning a completed revalidation form detailing teaching experience in an RYA-recognised centre. A minimum of 30 hours' teaching is required.
- If the certificate is more than two years out of date, the candidates will be expected to retake the course.
- If no teaching experience is logged, the applicant may be requested to attend a reassessment at their own cost.

RYA Advanced Powerboat Instructor Course

This course can be regarded as the top award within powerboat instruction. It is run at Recognised Training Centres by an RYA Powerboat Trainer.

Due to the candidates already being experienced Instructors, the course does not have a requirement to be moderated.

How to become an RYA Advanced Powerboat Instructor

There is no separate RYA Intermediate Instructor course. Candidates who pass the RYA Advanced Instructor course will be able to train both Intermediate and Advanced students.

Course prerequisites:

- The RYA Advanced Instructor course lasts two days and the minimum age is 18. It is run by an RYA Powerboat Trainer.

- Existing powerboat Instructors wishing to teach the Intermediate and Advanced Powerboat courses must hold the Advanced Powerboat Course Completion certificate, as well as one of the Advanced Powerboat Certificate of Competence, RYA Yachtmaster Coastal (Power) Certificate of Competence or RYA Yachtmaster (Offshore) Power Certificate of Competence, and attend a two-day Advanced Instructor Endorsement Course.

- Please note that if you will be teaching the Advanced course you should hold one of the following certificates of competence with a valid commercial endorsement: Advanced Powerboat, or RYA Yachtmaster Coastal (Power), or RYA Yachtmaster (Offshore) Power.

Course trainers may ask for candidates to provide evidence of logged teaching hours.

The course will last for two days and one evening, which will include a night exercise conducted in darkness.

Syllabus

The course content includes how to train and coach the following aspects:

- Practical boat handling in a variety of situations.
- Daytime navigation, theory and practical.
- Navigating in darkness, theory and practical.
- Meteorology.
- Collision regulations, theory and practical application.
- Use of engines – including twin-engine installations.
- Emergency situations – including search patterns and helicopter rescue.
- Boat and crew 'management' both day and night.
- Effective delivery of all aspects of the RYA Advanced Powerboat course.

During the course, the trainer will be looking for the following to be demonstrated by the candidates:

- A well-developed awareness of safety in all aspects of powerboating.
- A thorough knowledge of the activity.
- Effective communication skills.
- Ability to design stimulating and challenging exercises for potential students.
- Being 'in-charge' of any given situation or exercise whilst allowing students to develop their own leadership skills in a supportive environment.
- Ability to assess students' strengths and weaknesses.
- Ability to deliver effective feedback in an encouraging, sympathetic and supportive manner.

RYA Powerboat Trainer

The RYA Powerboat Trainer is an experienced RYA Advanced Powerboat Instructor who trains and assesses Instructors at all levels within the powerboat scheme.

Those who would like to be considered as trainers should contact their Regional Development Officer or Coach to ascertain their suitability. They should then complete an application form for the course. Overseas candidates should contact RYA head office directly.

If approved, they will then be invited to attend a selection day to demonstrate their suitability. This course will test their general boating knowledge, their practical ability in boat handling and their navigation skills, day and night.

Successful applicants will then be invited onto the training course, where they will receive training in all the necessary aspects required to train successfully RYA Powerboat and RYA Advanced Powerboat Instructors.

The RYA Safety Boat Course

There is at present no formal course for training RYA Powerboat Instructors to be RYA Safety Boat Instructors. If an RYA Powerboat Instructor holds the RYA Safety Boat award, then they are able to instruct the RYA Safety Boat course. The rationale for this is that the Instructor has been trained to teach powerboating, holds the RYA Safety Boat award and has the knowledge and experience of the elements required. This is considered sufficient and suitable for them to be able to teach the award.

However, teaching the RYA Safety Boat course is distinctly different from teaching the other skills within the Level 2 award and, as such, requires a different approach. Instructors may find themselves teaching up to six candidates in two powerboats, so they must be satisfied that the students' boat-handling skills are sound and reliable.

The course requires a high degree of organisation and specialised equipment to offer the students and it will require careful consideration as to how the various craft used on the course are going to be positioned for the students to practise on them. Often, large activity and watersports centres and clubs will be best suited to providing the resources required.

RYA Powerboat Instructor to RYA Personal Watercraft Instructor Conversion

The Instructor conversion route to RYA Personal Watercraft Instructor ceased on 31 December 2023.

RYA Yachtmaster Instructor (Power) to RYA Powerboat Instructor Conversion

YMI(P)s with the relevant experience may convert to a PBI by ensuring the following:

- Hold a current, valid RYA Powerboat Level 2 award.
- Have at least two years' experience driving smaller sports boats or RIBs.
- Attend a one-day conversion course run by an RYA Powerboat Trainer.

The emphasis of the course is to adapt the knowledge and teaching style of the candidate to the RYA Powerboat Scheme and will contain the following elements:

- Familiarisation with the RYA Powerboat Level 1 and 2 syllabi and the level of knowledge required, including navigation theory.
- The importance, value and necessity of demonstrations whilst teaching.
- Awareness of and successful management of the time constraints of an RYA Powerboat Level 2 course.

Throughout the course, candidates must be able to demonstrate the following:

- Use of 'neutral' as a gear during low-speed manoeuvring.
- 'One hand steer, one hand gear' at all times.
- Wearing of a 'kill cord' at all times.
- Use of 'directed thrust' that outboard engines provide.

Successful candidates will receive a PBI certificate.

Note that there is no conversion to RYA Powerboat Advanced Instructor.

The RYA Powerboat Scheme

The RYA Powerboat Scheme was developed to provide a qualification for dinghy sailing instructors and club safety boat drivers using powerboats to cover their dinghy fleets. It has grown from that original concept into what is now the most popular scheme that the RYA offers. Thousands of students annually take part in training to gain an RYA Powerboat award both here in the UK and now overseas at one of the many Recognised Training Centres worldwide.

The scheme is applicable to sportsboats, RIBs, dories and launches, and boats that don't provide accommodation and cooking facilities.

The lowest age limit for RYA training in powerboats is eight years old (RYA Powerboat Level 1 only).

Eight to eleven-year-olds should only use powered craft under the supervision of a responsible adult on board.

The minimum age for an RYA Powerboat Level 2 course is 12 years old. Those aged 12–16 should only use powered craft under the supervision of a responsible adult.

Certificates issued to those younger than 16 should be endorsed appropriately.

RYA Powerboat Scheme Structure

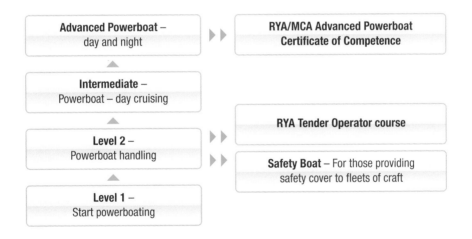

RYA Powerboat Level 2 – Powerboat Handling

The RYA Powerboat Level 2 course is designed to teach boat handling and seamanship in either planing or displacement boats. The course may be taken by novices new to boating, as no previous knowledge is required, although it would be of benefit if students had previous experience.

The course will be run over two days by an RYA Powerboat Instructor. The course will run from an RYA-recognised school. The minimum age for participants is 12 years old. Certificates for those aged 12–16 will be endorsed to the effect that they should only use powered craft under the supervision of a responsible adult.

The ratio of students to Instructor should not exceed 3:1.

This is a practical course and teaching should emphasise this, with a minimum of 75 per cent being afloat.

Instructor will deliver the course to 3 different levels of teaching. These levels are:

- **Knowledge of the subject**
- **Understands the subject**
- **Can demonstrate the required level of proficiency**

Golden Rules for Instructing

As with most instructing, there are some fundamental points that the Instructor should follow when teaching students. These should be instilled in the student from the beginning, so that they become habitual and stay with the student whenever they are driving boats. They support the routine checks that are made before embarking.

- **Killcord.** This could be considered the most important piece of safety equipment onboard a small powerboat. It should be worn by the helm at all times, preferably around the leg. If the helm were to fall from the helm position, or worse overboard, the engine will be stopped immediately, preventing the boat from continuing not under control. Every time someone takes up the helm position, the killcord should be attached before the engine is started.

- **Spare killcord.** If the helm is unfortunate enough to fall overboard, they will stop the engine if they are wearing the killcord correctly. However, it means that they have taken the killcord with them. In order for the remaining crew to be able to restart the engine to recover the helm, they will need a spare killcord. It should either be placed in a position of prominence, or every crew member should be aware of where it is stowed.

- **'Propeller check'.** Before the engine is started, a crew member (or helm) should take a visual check over the transom and inspect the area around the propeller for unwanted obstructions or debris.

- **'Tell-tale check'.** After the engine is started, a crew member (or helm) should check to see that the tell-tale jet is operating normally. If not, the engine should be switched off and the cause investigated.

- **'One hand gear, one hand steer'.** This hand position should be taught so that the student always has control of the steering but, more importantly, control of the throttle/gear selector. It would not prevent the lever being accidentally knocked, but it would allow the helm to bring it immediately back to the neutral position.

- **Crew position.** Before moving off, the helm should ensure that all the crew members are positioned correctly. This would normally be sitting on the seats provided and holding on with at least one hand.

- **Alerting crew.** Before any manoeuvre is performed, the helm should warn crew of their intentions. A simple 'power up', 'turn to port' will suffice.

- **Instructor position.** (For teaching purposes only). The Instructor should position themselves where they can easily reach the two main controls quickly. If they are teaching correctly they may never need to do so, but it's important that they can.

- **Changing helm.** When changing helm, the Instructor should ensure the boat is in a safe position to do so.

Level 1 – Start Powerboating

This course is to provide a practical introduction to boat handling and safety in powerboats. It can be taken in planing or displacement boats and the certificate issued will be endorsed to indicate the type of boat in which training took place.

The course duration is for one day only. The minimum age for students is eight years old and the certificate for this age group will be endorsed so that 8–11-year-olds should only use powered craft under the supervision of a responsible adult on board the craft.

Instructors must use a dual killcord system that is worn by the Instructor and student.

There is not a specific section for Level 1. However, the elements included within the course can be found in Level 2. Instructors can refer to the relevant sections for guidance.

Boat Preparation

Aim: To ensure that the boat is ready to embark.

Before a boat is launched or taken away from its berth, the boat and its crew must be equipped and prepared for what will follow. This should include the regular items needed afloat to allow the crew and their boat to function and carry out any tasks or duties. It also includes being prepared for any emergency situations that may be encountered. Put simply, the boat and crew must be as self-sufficient as possible.

Success indicator: The boat is fully prepared with all fluid levels checked; controls and electrical equipment all functioning as intended; all lines coiled and secured; all safety and boat equipment stowed and secured and the engine running; cooling jet functioning and running temperature satisfactory.

Planning

- Crew – clothing; protective clothing (waterproofs/drysuits); PFDs (lifejackets/buoyancy aids correctly fitted); appropriate footwear; crew briefing.
- Boat – Killcord/spare killcord; lines/warps; fenders; fuel; tools; VHF; flares; anchor; chain and warp; alternative means of propulsion; compass; first aid kit; horn; GPS/plotter; baler; hull/tubes integrity (see RYA Recognition Guidance Notes for full list).
- Safe and effective stowage of gear.
- Starting engine (propeller check; area/crew clear; start engine; check cooling water tell-tale).
- Engine and controls operating as to manufacturer's guidelines.
- Killcord functioning correctly.
- Steering functioning correctly.

In addition to preparing the boat and crew, a 'plan of the day' should be created. This does not need to be long and complicated, but ought to be considered before setting out.

Factors to address are:

- Boat and equipment (as above).
- Crew (as above).
- A passage plan; destination; alternative destination (plan B); timings/distances; ETA/ETD; shore contact; chart information.
- Weather – obtain an accurate, up-to-date forecast for the area being used.
- Tide – if operating in a tidal venue obtain tidal information for the duration of operation (and either side of it).
- Launching/recovery (if necessary).

Launching

Aim: To launch the boat safely and successfully, usually using a vehicle and slipway.

Success indicator: The boat is in the water and under control in a position where it can be boarded by the crew safely without causing damage or injury to either. The launching vehicle and trailer are positioned safely away from the slip and not causing an obstruction to other slip users.

Planning

Prior to launching the boat a series of pre-launch checks should be carried out. These will include:

- Park vehicle and trailer on flat, level ground away from the vicinity of the slipway while checks are carried out. This means that the slipway won't be blocked.

- Check any local bylaws and regulations for the launch site. If the slipway is manned, check that launching can take place and pay any fees that are due. This should be checked prior to arrival.

- Check the condition of the slipway and gradient. It is nearly always possible to launch a boat as gravity will assist, but recovery may prove more difficult.

- Check where the vehicle will be parked (including the trailer).

- Decide on where and how the boat will be left once it is in the water. For this reason, it is often better to launch multi-handed rather than single-handed. Agree on what hand signals are to be used.

- If the journey has been a long one, allow the wheel bearings on the trailer to cool down.

- Remove all transit straps that have been used to secure the boat to the trailer, but ensure that the winch strap and safety back-up are securely fastened.

- Remove the trailer (lighting) board and stow.

- Check and replace all/any bungs.

- Check fuel. This should be checked before setting off.

- If possible, briefly start and run the engine to ensure correct operation. This will require a water supply and the correct equipment to introduce running water into the engine's cooling system. This is a good time to check the killcord operation.

- Safety equipment and other sundries can be stowed aboard now, but this does add weight. It might be better to stow it onboard after the launch.

Approach

- Reverse the vehicle and trailer down the slipway.

- Ensure all those that are associated with the launch are well clear of the vehicle and trailer and are clearly in the vision of the vehicle driver.

- Check that the vehicle can recover the boat and trailer at this point.

- Continue reversing down the slip until the trailer wheels are near the water.

- If a crew member (or Instructor, when training is taking place) is going to drive the boat off the trailer, they can get in at this point. Ensure that the trailer and vehicle are stationary, preferably with the wheels chocked, before getting onboard.

Manoeuvre

- Reverse the boat into the water until it starts to float.
- If the above won't happen without immersing the vehicle, consider using a length of rope between the vehicle and trailer. This will require someone to guide the trailer as it is lowered into the water.
- Remove the winch and safety strap. While holding onto the painter, float the boat off the trailer. If a crewmember is onboard the craft, they can start the engine and drive it to a safe position.
- Swiftly remove the vehicle and trailer to parking spaces away from the head of the slipway.
- Consider rinsing the trailer wheel bearings at this point.

Escape

- On an unfamiliar slipway it is worth trying to recover (drive back up) the slipway before taking the boat all the way to the water's edge. It's better to find out if the vehicle can recover the boat sooner rather than later.

Recovery is almost the reverse of the method described above. Ensure the following:

- The trailer should be lowered into the water sufficiently for at least the bow of the craft to be positioned onto it.
- It can then be winched fully onto the trailer.
- In addition to securing the winch strap onto the craft, the safety strap should be securely fastened to the craft strong point (usually the 'D' ring for the painter).
- Once the trailer and boat have been removed from the water, but while still on a gradient, the bungs can be removed. Ensure that the vehicle and trailer cannot roll back down the slipway, preferably by chocking the trailer wheels. It is recommended that crew do not ride in the boat either during the launch or recovery stage in case of any gear failure.

Theory

Knowledge of:

- Use of a trailer or launching trolley. Some schools keep their boats afloat on a mooring or in a marina, therefore this section can be taught as a theory topic.
- Consideration of launching and prevailing sea conditions. These would include on/offshore wind, tide height, sea state and any local hazards or obstructions.
- The number of people required to launch. Two would be considered a safe minimum – one to drive the vehicle, the other to guide the driver and to deal with the boat once it is launched.
- Construction, gradient, width and the condition of the slipway. This would include provision for leaving the vehicle and trailer after launching.
- How to launch on steep and/or slippery slipways. Choice of vehicle, launching over a beach and the how to launch and recover from a lee shore.
- Care of the trailer, its fittings, bearings, lights, winch and lashings and lashing points.

Slow Speed Familiarisation

Aim: To introduce students to the boat, the controls and how it operates and behaves in a pressure-free environment.

Success indicator: Students can smoothly and effectively select gears (forward/reverse), drive the boat on a straight course, turn in either direction in forward and reverse, and bring the boat to a stop in the water using the elements (wind/tide) to assist.

Planning

- The Instructor should position the boat in a large open space clear of obstacles. Tide is not a consideration at this point.
- Practise engaging forward gear (or ahead) and returning to neutral. Gear shifts should be smooth and 'quiet'.
- Practise engaging reverse (or astern) and returning to neutral. Gear shifts should be smooth and 'quiet'.

Approach

- Once in gear ahead, practise steering (Top tip: **one hand steer**, **one hand gear**). Students should experience that steerage is effective only when in gear.
- Awareness of pivot points when steering (one-third back from the bow going ahead, one-third forward from the stern when going astern).
- Once in gear astern, practise speed control (taking care not to take in water over the transom), and steering.

Manoeuvre

- From moving ahead, practise bringing the boat to a 'standstill'. Use 'transits' to check that the boat is stopped. Practise going into and away from the elements to experience that the boat is likely only to stop travelling into the elements.
- When the boat has stopped, students can determine the 'direction of drift'. Students should then find that by pointing the boat into the elements the boat can be brought to a controlled 'stop'. Once this concept has been established, it can be used in a similar way for all subsequent manoeuvres.
- From going astern, practise bringing the boat to a standstill, using transits.

Escape

- As the boat is likely to be in an open and clear area, providing no other vessels enter the area, no escape action should be necessary.

Holding Off

Aim: To hold station in a designated space, likely to be in close proximity to a mooring buoy or post as a reference point.

Success indicator: The boat is held stationary, close to a fixed mark using steering and forward gear only. Casual observers would assume that the boat is moored to the mark.

Planning

- Use a suitable mark as a point to 'hold off'.
- Ensure it is clear of obstructions and other water users.
- Determine if there is any tidal flow/current around the mark.
- Establish 'direction of drift'.
- Decide on the distance to be used to hold off the mark.

Approach

- Position the bow into the direction of drift.
- Position the boat at the agreed distance off the mark.
- Ensure that the boat is 'stopped' in position.

Manoeuvre

- Observe the bow in relationship to the mark.
- Identify which way the bow is going to 'fall off' the mark.
- Apply opposite steering lock in relationship to the movement of the bow.
- Engage forward gear.
- The bow should swing back towards the mark.
- Engage neutral.
- Repeat the sequence above as necessary.
- Continue until the boat can be held on station with confidence.
- Reduce the distance from the mark as a development.
- Use neutral as a 'gear'. It is likely that neutral will be used more than ahead.
- Try to avoid using reverse.

Escape

- If the distance between the bow and the mark becomes too small, engage neutral gear.
- Allow the tide/current (or wind) to drift the boat away from the mark.
- Re-position the boat in the starting position.
- Repeat the exercise.

Picking up a Mooring

Aim: To pick up a mooring safely and attach a line (usually the painter).

Success indicator: The boat is brought to a halt immediately next to the mooring buoy with the buoy next to the side of the bow. Crew will easily be able to reach over and pick up the mark safely, tying on if necessary.

Planning

- Decide on which buoy is to be used.
- Establish if it is safe to do so and that any permission required is granted.
- Ensure that there are no underwater obstructions around the buoy.
- Establish if it has a 'pick-up' buoy that can be used.
- Decide on the direction of drift.
- Decide on where the buoy will be placed in relation to the bow.
- Check for other water users/hazards.
- Fully brief the crew on what tasks they are to perform.

Approach

- Position boat well below the direction of drift.
- Turn the bow towards the buoy.
- Begin the approach towards the buoy.
- Maintain slow approach speed. This will be best achieved by regular use of neutral.
- Position boat so that the selected side of the bow is towards the buoy.
- Check to ensure that there are no other water users/hazards present.
- As the distance between boat and buoy decreases, ensure that the approach speed is brought down to dead slow.
- Ensure that the crew is ready to pick up the mark.
- Have a boat hook ready if required.

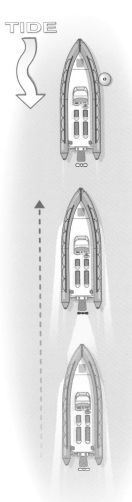

Manoeuvre

■ As the boat makes gentle contact with the buoy, the crew should reach over to pick up the buoy.

■ The boat should now be at a standstill.

■ If practising the manoeuvre, crew should take a turn onto the buoy to allow the mooring line to tension.

■ If the boat is to be left on the buoy, the painter should be made fast to the correct part of the mooring (not the pick-up handle).

Escape

■ If the boat is allowed to run out of 'way' and stop before the buoy then more drive can be applied by going ahead.

■ If the boat is carrying too much way and the boat makes contact with the mooring, engage neutral and allow the boat to drift past and away from the buoy. Do NOT engage gear until the boat is well clear of the mooring and its lines.

Leaving the Mooring

Planning

■ If the mooring was picked up as an exercise, the crew should hold the mooring until maximum tension comes onto the line. If practising in a standard teaching boat in normal tidal conditions, this should be feasible.

■ If the mooring is being left after a prolonged period, start the engine in readiness.

■ Ensure that it is clear astern.

■ Brief all crew as to their duties.

■ Check all around for other water users and hazards.

Approach

■ Brief crew to stand by to cast off.

■ Ensure again it is clear all round and particularly astern.

■ Issue the command 'cast off'.

■ Allow the boat to drift back.

■ Continue to ensure that it is clear all round.

Manoeuvre

- Continue to drift until the boat is well clear of the mooring.
- Once clear, apply steering lock towards clear water.
- Engage gear ahead.
- Drive to a safe position.

Escape

- If it is not clear or safe to do so, stay attached to the buoy.
- Do not cast off until it is clear to do so and the engine is functioning correctly.

Theory

Understands:

- Prior preparation of the mooring warp or painter.
- Use of a boat hook to extend reach (if required).
- Making fast (if not included in the exercise).

Coming Alongside a Jetty or Pontoon

Aim: To bring the boat safely alongside a solid pontoon without damage.

Success indicator: The boat approaches the pontoon slowly and comes to a halt as contact is made. The entire side of the boat (or its fenders) should make contact simultaneously.

There are four general ways of coming alongside and onto a pontoon. These four methods are determined by the prevailing conditions (direction of drift) present at the time. Tide is usually the strongest influence, so for reasons of clarity, tide will be used to illustrate all likely situations. In inland locations or where the tidal flow is weak, the wind may become the dominant element.

The four likely conditions are:

1. Tide running parallel to the chosen face (uptide).
2. Tide running parallel to the chosen face (downtide).
3. Tide running at 90 degrees onto chosen face.
4. Tide running at 90 degrees away from chosen face.

Tide Running Parallel to the Chosen Face

Planning

- Establish the direction of the tide.
- Position the boat downtide and away from the pontoon.
- Allocate crew tasks and brief accordingly.
- Prepare fenders, lines, boathook etc.
- Check for obstructions/other water users.
- Decide on what part of the pontoon to be used.
- Plan escape route.

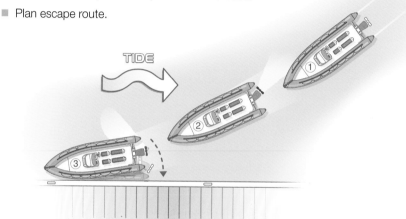

Approach

- From a position clear of the pontoon, begin a parallel approach into the tide.
- Maintain slow speed, but make progress against the tide.
- Continue to check for obstructions and other water users.
- When the course allows an approach angle to the pontoon of 40–45 degrees, turn towards the pontoon.
- Maintain the approach angle by using transits. Note that the bow of the boat might not be pointing directly at the pontoon at this stage.

Manoeuvre

- Ensure that the approach speed is slow – use neutral as a 'gear' to achieve this.
- When within 1–2 boat lengths from the pontoon, engage neutral.
- Turn the steering full lock away from the pontoon.
- Engage ahead gear briefly to push the stern of the boat towards the pontoon.

- Return to neutral.
- If the tide is weak or there is no wind/current, while in neutral apply opposite steering lock and use a small burst of astern to slow the boat and to draw the stern towards the pontoon. However, students should try not to rely routinely on using reverse as a 'brake'. Doing so would mean that the wind/tide/current are not being used to best effect.
- Attach lines (painter first).

Escape

- While approaching, keep checking for obstructions/other water users.
- During approach, if an escape route is needed, due to the approach course being at an angle (providing there is room) the boat can be turned safely away from the pontoon. Ensure that there is space for the stern to swing clear of the pontoon.
- Once within two boat lengths, either engage neutral to make gentle contact (approach speed should have been dead slow), or engage astern gear to draw back away from the vessel.

Leaving from Alongside a Pontoon

Planning

- Ensure that the engine is running.
- Allocate crew tasks and brief accordingly.
- Check for obstructions/other water users.
- Release all unnecessary lines.

Approach/Manoeuvre

Light tide:

- Release all lines except the painter.
- Turn the wheel full lock away from the pontoon.
- Check around and particularly astern.
- Cast off the painter.
- Engage astern gear.
- As the stern clears away from the pontoon, return the steering to amidships.
- Continue to draw away from the pontoon.
- When in clear space, engage neutral and then drive away in the desired direction.
- Bring in fenders and tidy down lines. Reposition crew.

Strong tide (alternative method):

- Release all lines except stern spring and painter.
- Position steering amidships.
- Cast off the painter.
- Allow the bow to 'pay off' due to the action of the tide.
- Wait for an angle of approximately 30 degrees.
- Cast off and recover stern spring.
- Engage ahead gear.
- Drive slowly away from pontoon into a clear space.
- Bring in fenders and tidy down lines, reposition crew.

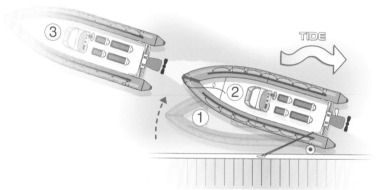

Theory

Understands:

- Preparation required of lines and fenders and the amount of each required for successful mooring alongside. The minimum required would be the painter, a stern line and fenders at the vulnerable points on the hull, particular the stern quarter.
- Attachment of lines and fenders on board. Lines should be tied onto purpose-built strong points, usually cleats. Lines can be spliced on or fastened with a knot that can be easily undone under load (round turn & two half hitches). Fenders are commonly tied on with a clove hitch.
- Stowage of lines and fenders when under way. All boats should have their lines coiled and stowed to keep them tidy and free from hazards. It also helps prevent lines from going overboard and possibly fouling the propeller.

Coming Alongside – Downtide Approach

Planning

- Establish the direction of the tide.
- Position the boat uptide and away from the pontoon.
- Allocate crew tasks and brief accordingly.
- Prepare fenders, lines, boathook etc.
- Check for obstructions/other water users.
- Decide on what part of the pontoon to be used.
- Plan escape route.

Approach

- From a position clear of the pontoon, begin a parallel approach into the tide. However, the boat should be closer in towards the pontoon than that of a conventional approach.
- Maintain slow speed, but make progress through the water to provide 'steerage'.
- Continue to check for obstructions and other water users.
- Turn to create an approach angle that is finer than that of 'against the tide' (approximately 15 degrees). This will bring the boat closer to the pontoon than usual.
- Maintain the approach angle using observation and transits.
- Use neutral as a gear to control approach speed.

Manoeuvre

- As the boat closes on the chosen point on the pontoon, select neutral.
- Apply steering lock towards the pontoon.
- Immediately select astern gear.
- This will slow the boat and draw the stern in towards the pontoon.
- Use steering to bring the boat alongside.
- Use throttle and gear to hold position while doing so.
- Make stern fast with stern line. Make fast other lines as necessary.

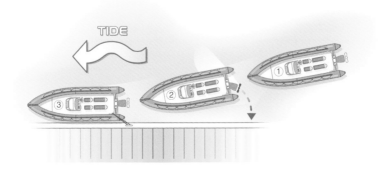

Escape

- Due to the finer angle and faster approach speed, be prepared to abandon the manoeuvre earlier than normal.
- If excessive contact is anticipated, apply steering lock away from the pontoon.
- Apply astern gear and draw the boat away from the pontoon.
- If steering is then applied, the boat can be held parallel to the pontoon.
- It may be possible then to 'ferry glide' back in towards the pontoon.

Leaving the Pontoon – Weak Tide

Planning

- Start engine.
- Plan action required to leave.
- Allocate crew tasks and brief accordingly.
- Check for obstructions and other water users.
- Plan escape.

Approach/Manoeuvre

- Cast off all lines except stern line.
- Apply steering lock away from the pontoon.
- Check all round, particularly astern.
- Cast off stern line.
- Immediately select astern gear.
- Allow stern to come away from the pontoon.
- Remain in astern and return steering to amidships.
- 'Ferry glide' the boat away from the pontoon.
- Once in clear space, select neutral and recover fenders, tidy down lines, reposition crew.
- Drive away in desired direction.

Escape

If there are obstructions or other water users, remain fast, alongside, until it is clear.

If the boat has moved away from the pontoon, it may be possible to remain in gear and apply steering lock back towards the pontoon.

Strong Tide – Alternative

Planning

- Start engine.
- Plan action required to leave.
- Allocate crew tasks and brief accordingly.
- Check for obstructions and other water users.
- Set steering to amidships.

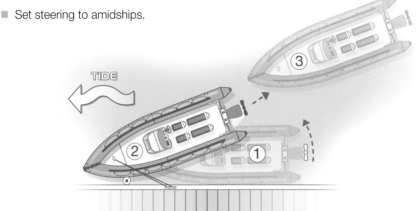

Approach/Manoeuvre

- Cast off all lines except forward spring and stern line.
- Cast off stern line.
- Allow the stern to 'pay off' and be swung away from the pontoon.
- Once an angle of 15–20 degrees is achieved, select astern.
- Cast off forward spring line.
- Allow the boat to be drawn away from the pontoon.
- Use steering to 'ferry glide' away from the pontoon.
- Once in clear space, select neutral and recover fenders, tidy down lines, reposition crew.
- Drive away in desired direction.

Escape

- If there are obstructions or other water users, remain fast, alongside, until it is clear.
- If the boat has begun manoeuvring and the stern line has been cast off, but the forward spring is still made fast, apply steering lock towards the pontoon and engage astern gear. The stern will swing back towards the pontoon.
- If the boat has moved away from the pontoon, it may be possible to remain in gear and apply steering lock back towards the pontoon.

Coming Alongside – Tide Flowing onto the Pontoon Face

Planning

- Establish the direction of the tide.
- Position the boat uptide and away from the pontoon.
- Allocate crew tasks and brief accordingly.
- Prepare fenders, lines, boathook etc.
- Check for obstructions/other water users.
- Decide on what part of the pontoon to be used.
- Plan escape route.

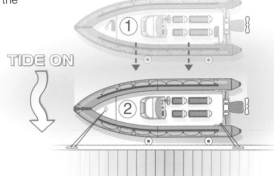

Approach

- From a location clear of the pontoon and uptide of it, manoeuvre the boat to opposite the selected position on the pontoon.
- Allow the tide to carry the boat sideways towards the pontoon.
- Continue to check for obstructions and other water users.
- Maintain a position parallel to the pontoon by using steering lock and forward and astern gear.

Manoeuvre

- The tide will continue to carry the boat towards the pontoon.
- The boat should make gentle contact with the pontoon.
- Make the boat fast with the appropriate lines.

Escape

- Continue to maintain a lookout for obstructions and other water users.
- If the manoeuvre needs to be aborted, apply ahead gear and drive the boat clear and away from the obstruction.

To Leave the Pontoon – Weak Tide

Planning

- Start engine.
- Plan action required to leave.
- Allocate crew tasks and brief accordingly.
- Check for obstructions and other water users.
- Plan escape.

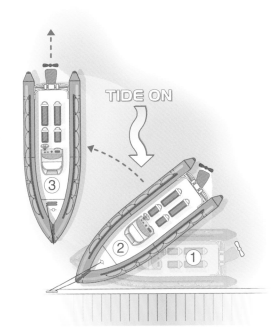

Approach

- Cast off all lines except the painter.
- Apply steering lock away from the pontoon.
- Check all round, particularly astern.

Manoeuvre

- Cast off painter.
- Select astern gear.
- Allow stern to come away from the pontoon.
- Continue going astern.
- Once in clear space, select neutral and recover fenders, tidy down lines, reposition crew.
- Drive away in desired direction.

Escape

- If there are obstructions or other water users, remain fast, alongside, until it is clear.
- If the boat has moved away from the pontoon, manoeuvre it back to a position parallel to the pontoon and allow the tide to return it to the pontoon.

Strong Tide – Alternative

Planning

- Start engine.
- Plan action required to leave.
- Allocate crew tasks and brief accordingly.
- Check for obstructions and other water users.
- Apply steering lock away from the pontoon.

Approach/Manoeuvre

- Cast off all lines except the painter. The painter should be set as a 'slip' line.
- Motor gently back until the painter becomes taut.
- Apply steering lock away from the pontoon.
- Engage astern gear.
- Allow the stern to be drawn away from the pontoon.
- Continue until the boat is 90 degrees to the pontoon.
- Alert crew that they are about to cast off.
- Engage neutral, cast off the painter and recover line.
- Engage astern gear and drive boat into a clear space, recover fenders, tidy down lines and reposition crew.

Escape

- If the boat has swung away from the pontoon but is still attached, simply apply gentle steering lock back towards the pontoon.

Coming Alongside – Tide Flowing away from Pontoon Face

Planning

- Establish the direction of the tide.
- Position the boat down tide and away from the pontoon.
- Allocate crew tasks and brief accordingly.
- Prepare fenders, lines, boathook etc.
- Check for obstructions/other water users.
- Decide on what part of the pontoon to be used.
- Plan escape route.

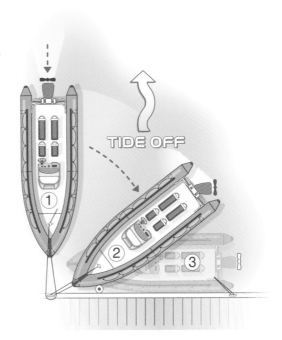

Approach

- From a location clear of the pontoon and downtide of it, position the boat opposite the selected place on the pontoon, bows pointing towards the chosen area.
- Make the painter ready.
- Continue to check for obstructions and other water users.
- Engage ahead gear and approach the pontoon, bows on.

Manoeuvre

- Approach the pontoon at dead slow speed.
- Once within reaching distance, engage neutral.
- Crew members drop the painter onto a cleat on the pontoon and make fast within the boat.
- Allow the boat to 'drop back' on the tide, applying tension to the painter.
- Once the painter is taut, apply full steering lock towards the pontoon.
- Engage astern gear.
- Allow the stern of the boat to be 'drawn' towards the pontoon.
- Once alongside, make the boat fast with the stern line.

Escape

- Continue to maintain a lookout for obstructions and other water users.
- To abort, cast off the painter and allow the boat to drift away with the tide. If the painter had not been attached, engage neutral and allow boat to drift away from the pontoon.

To Leave the Pontoon

Planning

- Start engine.
- Plan action required to leave.
- Allocate crew tasks and brief accordingly.
- Check for obstructions and other water users.
- Plan escape.

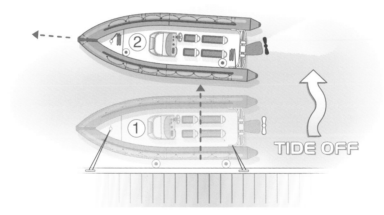

Approach/Manoeuvre

- Have a final all-round check.
- Alert crew that they are about to cast off.
- Cast off bow and stern lines simultaneously.
- Allow boat to drift away sideways, parallel to the pontoon.
- Once in clear space, recover fenders, tidy down lines, reposition crew.

Escape

- Remain alongside until the area is clear.

Turning in a Confined Space

Aim: To turn the boat in a space as close to its own length as possible, e.g. pontoons within a marina.

Success indicator: The boat is turned as close to 'on the spot' as possible, with no discernible distance travelled either forwards or backwards.

This task is best practised initially in an open space using marker buoys or transits to mark the limit of the area. Once mastered, it can be practised in more limited areas.

Planning

- Position boat in a clear space.
- Ensure boat is stopped in the water.
- Check for obstructions and other water users.
- Assess the direction of drift.

Top Tips

- Steer before gear.
- Due to the rotation of the propeller, or 'prop walk', most boats turn best clockwise.
- Any application of power done into the direction of drift can be done for a little longer than one done away from it.
- Imagine anywhere upwind/tide as the 'safe zone'. Anywhere downwind/tide is the 'danger zone'.

Approach/Manoeuvre

- Apply full steering lock (preferably to starboard).
- Engage ahead gear.
- Once the boat begins to gather way (use transits), engage neutral.
- Apply full opposite lock (to port).
- Check all around, particularly astern.
- Apply astern gear.
- Once boat starts to gather way (use transits), engage neutral.
- Repeat the above sequence until the boat has turned sufficiently.

Escape

- Keep a good all-round lookout.
- If another water user approaches, use appropriate action according to the International Regulations for Preventing Collisions at Sea (IRPCS).
- If the boat is approaching an obstruction, and it is prudent to do so, use **gentle** power and steering to take the boat away from it. If contact is likely or inevitable, at this point DO NOT try to power away. Select neutral and allow gentle contact to be made. Use a 'roving' fender between the boat and obstacle, if possible. Once the boat has settled, use the necessary action to extricate the boat safely and with no damage. Reposition accordingly.

Man Overboard

Aim (primary): To be aware and understand that 'prevention is better than cure' i.e. it is better not to have a crew member (or helm) in the water than to have to carry out an MOB manoeuvre.

Aim (secondary): To be able to recover a person safely (a dummy only for the purpose of the exercise) from the water.

Success indicator: After a 'dead slow' approach, the boat is brought to a complete halt next to the dummy with the engine turned off. Crew can then recover the dummy safely.

To achieve this, the following simple actions will help prevent a crew member going overboard while under way:

■ Crew should remain seated and holding on while under way. Ideally, they should be sitting on a purpose-built seat with a backrest and facility for holding on with at least one hand. Should the crew need to move from this position to carry out their duties, they should follow the adage of 'one hand for the crew – one hand for the boat'. The helm and crew need to communicate their intentions.

■ The helm must drive the boat so as not to place the crew or themselves (or other water users) in any danger. If crew members are out of their seats and moving around the boat, then the boat must be driven with the utmost caution and not in a manner that would place the crew in harm's way.

Man overboard is taught as a 'drill' using a 'dummy' target to simulate a crew member falling overboard. The drill must **never** be taught with real people.

Two main methods of MOB drill are taught.

Upwind Method

Tide is not a consideration as the boat and MOB are in the same patch of moving water.

Planning

■ In a clear area that will not interfere with other water users, crew prepares to throw over the MOB dummy.

■ Although the MOB is a drill, as far as is reasonable the helm and crew should treat it as an emergency situation.

Approach

- When safe to do so, crew throws the dummy target overboard.
- All call 'man overboard' to alert the helm of the situation.
- Those who are able and safe to do so point at the MOB target.
- Helm will hold their course and reduce speed smoothly to 'dead slow'.
- Crew if they are able and helm if they are not simulate a distress alert/'Mayday' call to the Coastguard.
- The boat (travelling at slow speed) should be brought around well downwind of the target dummy to begin an upwind approach.
- If crew members are present and able, they should prepare either a line or boathook to assist in reaching the dummy. They should do so without endangering themselves.

Manoeuvre

- Continue to approach the dummy. Speed should be 'dead slow'.
- Using neutral and ahead gears, continue a dead slow approach.
- The boat should be positioned so that the dummy is presented to one side of the bow, on the 'shoulder' between the bow and gunwale. Ideally, this should be the opposite side to the throttle, to prevent it being accidentally knocked by crew moving in the boat.
- The helm should be keeping a lookout while observing the dummy and the crew about to retrieve it.
- As the crew make a move with arm, boathook or line to retrieve the dummy, the helm should engage neutral if not already done (the boat should be stopped at this point) and immediately turn the engine **off** (turn off ignition key/remove killcord).
- Crew then retrieves the dummy.

Escape

- The helm should be very aware of their approach speed towards the dummy.
- If they are unhappy with the speed or direction of their approach, the helm should abort their approach early by selecting neutral and allow the boat to drift back away from the dummy.
- The boat can then be repositioned for another attempt.

N.B. Most students approach the MOB too quickly and arrive at the dummy with 'way' on the boat. Regular use of neutral while approaching the target should be encouraged to keep speed to a minimum.

Downwind (drift) Method

Ignore tide for the reason given above.

Planning

- In a clear area that will not interfere with other water users, crew prepares to throw over the MOB dummy.
- Although the MOB is a drill, as far as is reasonable the helm and crew should treat it as an emergency situation.

Approach

- When safe to do so, crew throws the dummy target overboard.
- All call 'man overboard' to alert the helm of the situation.
- Those who are able and safe to do so point at the MOB target.
- Helm will hold their course and reduce speed smoothly to 'dead slow'.
- Crew if they are able and helm if they are not simulate a distress alert/'Mayday' call to the Coastguard.
- The boat, travelling at slow speed, should be brought around upwind of the dummy, approximately two boat lengths away.
- The helm positions the boat across the wind and at 90 degrees to the dummy.
- With the engine still running, the helm assesses their drift down onto the dummy.
- If they suspect that the boat will miss the dummy while drifting, they are able to reposition using small inputs of power either ahead or astern.
- Crew prepares to reach for the dummy.

Manoeuvre

- The helm may repeat the above procedure while drifting until they are approximately two boat lengths away from the dummy.
- They then turn the engine off when they are certain they will reach them, but no later than on contact.
- The boat will continue to drift towards the target. The crew can be ready to make contact with the dummy.
- If the helm suspects that the boat will miss the target, a paddle can be used to reposition it.
- The boat will make soft contact with the dummy, which can then be retrieved.

Escape

■ Once the drift has been established, if it is between two and six boat lengths, the helm is safe to drive away on a straight course to reposition.

■ Once within two boat lengths, the engine should not be restarted until the crew member is brought aboard unless the boat and its entire crew are placed in danger.

N.B. This method is slower to carry out than the upwind method. However, this disadvantage is by far outweighed by the fact that the engine is turned off well away from the dummy and wind power alone is used to move the boat towards it. This removes the possibility of a propeller strike. This method should be considered if the person in the water is conscious and able to function normally. While closing on the MOB, they can be reached for with a heaving line and or boathook/paddle.

Theory

Knowledge of:

■ The various methods of recovering a crew member from the water with due consideration for the safety of the crew member in the water and the crew on the craft. Recovering a person from the water presents its own problems to the crew. Due to the manual handling issues it presents, great care should be taken to prevent injury to either the person being recovered or the crew performing the recovery.

Understands:

■ The effects of cold shock. Cold shock cannot be prevented, but if crew members are aware of the symptoms and they find themselves in the water, they can take steps to reduce the effects until the symptoms subside.

Anchoring

Aim: To anchor the boat in a safe and clear area.

Anchoring is used to fix the boat in a position where it is safe and will not cause damage to itself or other water users. It is often used when there are no moorings available, although anchoring in the vicinity of moorings is not recommended, as the anchor may become snagged in the 'ground tackle' of the other moorings.

Anchoring can also be carried out in an emergency situation e.g. engine failure, to fix the position of the boat and prevent it from drifting into danger.

Success indicator: The boat is lying at anchor directly over a chosen spot with the correct amount of scope paid out for the depth of water. The load on the anchor line is taken up on the boat on a point designed for this purpose. Due consideration has been given for the prevailing and expected conditions.

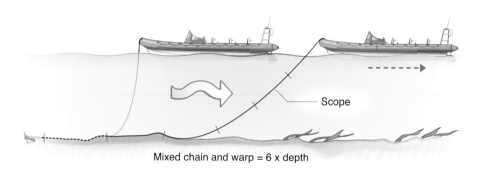

Scope

Mixed chain and warp = 6 x depth

Planning

- Decide on where the boat is to be anchored.
- Ensure that the area is safe, sheltered and clear of obstructions and channels.
- Take into account that the boat will swing through an arc while at anchor, so may swing towards other anchored/moored craft.
- Also take into account the state of the tide to prevent 'drying', or alternatively lifting the anchor out as the tide rises. Also, if the tide turns, the boat may swing through 180 degrees and face in the opposite direction.
- Check chart information to ensure that anchoring is permitted in that area and that the ground is not 'foul'.
- Brief crew and allocate tasks.
- Take the anchor out of the locker and 'flake down' the anchor line. Ensure that the end of the anchor line is made fast to the boat, or that it will be during the anchoring procedure.

Approach

■ Approach the spot to anchor over as if for mooring, i.e. into the direction of drift.

■ Drive into the direction of drift beyond the spot where the boat will rest once anchored.

■ Check depth (chart information or echo sounder).

■ Bring boat to a stop (use transits).

Manoeuvre

■ Lower the anchor carefully overboard from the bow, counting how much warp (scope) has been let out (an 'arm's length' is an accurate enough unit).

■ Feel for the anchor reaching the ground.

■ Allow the boat to begin drifting back.

■ As the boat drifts, let out the correct amount of scope for the depth (x4 for chain, x6 for warp).

■ 'Bend on' the painter to the anchor warp.

■ Allow the slack warp to be 'taken up'.

■ If required, briefly 'go astern' to dig the anchor in (snubbing).

■ Check that the anchor is holding by using 'transits'.

■ If it's not an exercise, stop the engine.

Escape

■ If the area doesn't appear suitable, choose another spot.

■ If the anchor isn't holding, 'snub' the anchor a little more and recheck.

■ If it's still not holding, it will need to be recovered (see next section) and relaid, probably in a different spot, with more warp (scope).

■ Avoid anchoring in a doubtful area, but if there is no choice, attach a 'trip' line to the tripping point on the anchor to aid recovery.

Recovery

Planning

■ Start the engine.

■ Brief crew and allocate tasks.

■ Plan escape.

■ Make all-round check.

Approach

- Motor **very** gently ahead.
- Crew takes in scope over the bow.
- Helm must ensure that they do not drive over the scope. Communicate with the crew throughout to avoid this situation.
- When the scope is straight 'up & down', engage neutral.

Manoeuvre

- Crew 'breaks out' the anchor and continues to retrieve scope and anchor.
- Once the anchor is aboard and crew members are positioned safely, the boat can be driven gently in desired direction.
- If safe to do so, crew members tidy and stow scope and anchor, then reposition themselves.

Escape

- If any obstructions/water users become apparent and in close proximity, engage neutral and make fast the anchor line until it becomes clear again.
- If the boat passes over the scope, **immediately** engage neutral and wait until the boat drifts back and the scope becomes clearly visible once again.

Theory

Knowledge of:

- The various types of anchor commercially available. There are several types available that would suit the sports boat operator. The type chosen will depend upon the holding ground being anchored into, budget, space available and the type of line or chain being used.
- The applications of various anchors and their holding power. See above.
- Stowage of anchor onboard the craft and how it would be attached. As anchors are heavy, they will cause damage if they can move about while the boat is under way. Therefore they should be stowed securely in a specific space aboard.
- The advantage of chain/warp and the ratio/amount required for each. Chain helps increase the holding power of an anchor, as it will provide a more horizontal pull. However, it is very heavy to stow onboard a small sportsboat. Therefore, rope or warp becomes a more suitable alternative. A compromise is to have a length of chain attached directly to the anchor, then warp attached to this.

Planing-speed Manoeuvres

Aim: To drive the boat safely at higher (planing) speeds and perform manoeuvres while doing so.

Most modern sportsboats and RIBs will plane easily, as they are designed to do so. Helmsmen need to be aware of the capabilities and limitations of their craft and also themselves while travelling at speed.

Research has proven that travelling at high speeds in a boat places huge loads on the occupants. If it is intended to travel at speed, it is vital that consideration is given to the positioning of the occupants. Ideally, they should be seated on a purpose-built seat and facing forward with good hand-holds.

Success indicator: The boat and crew are able to travel safely and efficiently at planing speed without causing damage or injury to either with due regard for the prevailing conditions. IRPCS are applied throughout.

Planning

- Stow and/or secure all loose equipment, including lines.
- Ensure that all crew are positioned correctly.
- Brief crew. Ensure that a good, all-round lookout is kept.
- Decide and agree on any signals to be used – verbal communication will be difficult or impossible at speed.
- Ensure that it is safe to proceed at speed in the given area. Aspects such as visibility, water conditions, other water users, collision regulations, restricted areas/channels etc. should all be taken into consideration.
- If the engine has a trim option, trim it fully down/in.

Approach/Manoeuvre

- Ensure that it is clear to proceed.
- Engage ahead gear and apply power.
- Once planing, reduce power sufficiently to allow the boat to continue to plane.
- Trim the engine up/out to attain the optimum attitude in the water.

Turning at Planing Speed

- In order to maintain 'grip' with the propeller and hull during a turn, trim the engine in/down before turning.
- Warn crew of intentions. Crew should be holding on.
- Make an all-round visual check, particularly in the direction of the coming turn.
- As the boat turns, it will slow down. Slight additional power may be added to maintain the chosen speed.

- Continue to keep a sharp all-round lookout.
- Once the turn is complete, trim the engine out/up and re-establish the required course.
- Remember – one hand steer, one hand gear.

Slowing Down

- Warn crew of intentions.
- Ensure it is clear all around, including directly behind.
- Trim engine in/down.
- Gently reduce power.
- As the boat 'drops' off the plane, ensure that the stern wave doesn't swamp the boat over the transom. Maintain some 'way' to avoid this.

Escape

- Keep a good, all-round lookout.
- Apply the IRPCS in good time.
- If in doubt, reduce power to allow the boat to proceed at a safe speed.
- Avoid sudden and violent manoeuvres.

Trim

At speed, a boat/engine can be 'trimmed' to achieve optimum performance and fuel economy. The general principle is to reduce the 'wetted area' of the boat in contact with the water. The smaller the area, the less power is needed to drive the boat forward.

The disadvantage of this is that the propeller is closer to the surface of the water so is prone to 'ventilation', where air is drawn down to the blades, causing a loss of 'grip'. In addition, the hull also has less grip on the water, so can 'skip' during turns.

Each boat will be different depending on its hull and engine, so it is recommended to practise and become familiar with the boat and its characteristics in calm, safe conditions.

RYA Powerboat Level 2 Theory

Knowledge of:

- **The various types of craft available.** Popular types are RIBs; dories; displacement launches; catamarans; speed/sportsboats; planing fishers (often with wheelhouses); and small cruisers (with accommodation).

- **The advantages and disadvantages of the different hulls and their respective sea-keeping abilities.** All the above craft have advantages and disadvantages. Before purchase, the owner should be clear as to what use they would like their boat to perform.

- **Seating arrangements onboard.** To ensure maximum crew safety and comfort, crew should be seated, facing forward with a handgrip available.

- **Stepped hulls and their use.** These hulls offer race-level performance when matched with the correct engine and drive. However, they are expensive and are only required for those that require the maximum performance from their craft.

- **Engines and drives.** The advantages and disadvantages of outboard, inboard, jet and outdrive engines, single and twin engine set-ups, the choice and use of different fuels.

- **The siting of fuel tanks, lines, batteries and wiring.** If buying a used or completed new boat, the owner may have no choice in where ancillaries are positioned. If buying a brand new, unfitted boat, they can have these items positioned to meet their requirements.

- **Fire extinguishers, their usefulness and siting.** These can be fitted for ease of access, and/or if the boat has a dedicated engine compartment it can have an automatic deployment system.

- **Routine engine maintenance, basic regular checks, simple fault diagnosis.** Students should develop a regular routine to ensure that all basic maintenance and checks are carried out.

- **Shutting/closing-down procedure.** As above.

- **Use and limitations of GPS units and chart plotters.** Students need to be aware of the differences between the two units and how to operate them.

- **Bylaws and local regulations.** Students should be made aware of the sources of information from websites and/or publications for a particular area.

- **Sources of relevant weather information.** As a minimum, a marine inshore forecast for the area to be used and for the day in question should be obtained.

- **Insurance.** Marine insurance, although not mandatory, is highly recommended for all boat users.

- **Boat registration schemes.** For example, in the UK the RYA SafeTrx service holds registration details for use by HM Coastguard if they need to mount a search and rescue operation if the vessel gets into difficulty.

Understands:

- **Awareness of other water users and the responsibilities of both.** Powerboaters share the water with many other water users. An understanding of the IRPCS is the starting point to avoiding accidents, but respect for others whether recreational or commercial is an accepted part of boating.

- **Communication with other craft by visual and electronic means.** Marine VHF is now the accepted norm when communicating with other craft. Training in its use and obtaining the correct certification is recommended. Visual signals are only effective over very short distances and, as such, should not be wholly relied on.

- **Disabled craft and how to deal with them, if required. Actions taken by disabled craft and being towed. Attachment of lines in both vessels. Agreement of terms.** Boaters have a well-deserved reputation for assisting others who have problems. This could involve a simple tow. Before undertaking this, though, consideration should be given as to what type of tow (astern or alongside), what strong points are to be used (bridle and painter), how far the tow will be for, and what terms for the tow have been decided upon before the tow commences.

- **Emergency action and action to prevent sinking.** Emergencies take many forms. Equipment is carried to help deal with these eventualities, but not all can be met. Sinking is a serious situation, but difficult to make contingency plans for. Soft wooden bungs and a mallet can be used for small breaches of the hull, but a larger one might require taking the craft to shallow water so it can take to the ground to prevent loss.

- **Being adrift and alternative means of propulsion (and its limitations).** If a vessel is disabled and adrift, the first action of the crew should be to fix its position by anchor so that it can't drift into danger. The crew then has some 'thinking time' to try and resolve the situation. Summoning help (by VHF call or attracting attention by visual means) may be of use. The craft might be moved by alternative means of propulsion, but in reality this is often a pair of paddles. Crew should be aware that they have very limited effectiveness.

- **Fire precautions and fighting fires, and the limitations and effectiveness of the equipment available.** Small, commercially available fire extinguishers, despite being designed for dealing with small blazes, are in reality limited in their effectiveness. Crew should be aware of these limitations. Having multiple extinguishers will contribute to a more successful outcome.

- **Distress signals and the various equipment available, means of issuing distress, DSC and the Mayday call.** RYA Powerboat Level 2 candidates are not required to hold a Marine VHF Operator's Certificate, but they should be made aware of the benefits and the means of obtaining one.

- **Advice for craft in limited visibility and the action they should take.** The RYA Powerboat Level 2 award is for small powerboats that are generally not equipped to operate in restricted visibility. However, these vessels can seek the relative safety of shallow waters in restricted visibility. This will take them away from areas of larger commercial shipping that are equipped for navigating more safely in poor visibility.

- **Charts, chart symbols, buoyage systems.** Being able to make use of the information contained on charts, where to find further information and the significance of buoys.

- **Tides and tidal streams.** Causes, effects and predictions from various sources.

- **Pilotage and passage planning.** The creation of a working plan and the notation used.

Can:

- Although contained within the theory section, students should be able to apply IRPCS, particularly rules 5, 7, 8, 9, and 12–18. Instruction should concentrate on the spirit and practical application of the rules, rather then memorising the numbers and content exactly.

- **Use a steering and hand bearing compass.** A steering compass is the fixed compass fitted to a boat, usually in front of the helm position. This will give the helm a clear view of the compass and, therefore, the heading of the boat. In order to drive on the chosen bearing, the helm will need to turn the boat until the bearing appears on the 'lubbers line'. Like any compass, the steering compass will be affected by any ferrous metal and electrical activity in proximity to it. To compensate, it will need either a correction card created for it, or it will need to be professionally corrected. Hand bearing compasses, by contrast, are not fixed and can be used anywhere in the boat and not just by the helm. Because of this, they can be used in an area well away from the interference that the fixed compass may suffer from. However, because of this, they cannot be 'adjusted'.

Boat Handling Theory

Knowledge of:

- **Loading and the effect that a load can have on the boat's handling and performance, its balance and trim.** Small boats are sensitive to how a load is distributed about them, and crew can also be considered as a load. In general terms, the boat should be balanced side to side and trimmed flat fore and aft. Crew can be easily moved and positioned to achieve the optimum attitude.

- **The significance of the CE mark and the manufacturer's recommendation on load and engine size/power.** New boats are obliged to carry a maker's plate on the stern/transom. This will give guidance on the maximum load permitted to be carried and the maximum power of the engine to be fitted.

- **The different handling characteristics of a displacement boat with rudder steering and shaft-driven propeller.** This type of set-up is usually found on displacement boats. They handle very differently to boats with outboards, even at slow speeds. They carry their way further, respond more slowly to steering input and steer very vaguely in reverse. However, once these differences have been learned, they can be positioned with the same accuracy as any other boat.

Understands:

- **Crew members and their welfare, positioning, the minimum number on faster craft, and their role in keeping a good lookout.** Although they may not be directly occupied once under way, the crew members are an important consideration in any boat. They are also useful in keeping a good lookout to assist the helm.

- **The importance of boat control in waves and rough water.** Rough water exerts adverse effects on the boat and crew. Care must be taken when driving in such conditions.

- **The importance of adequate seating and minimising the possibility of injury or ejection.** Having the correct seating and handholds onboard can reduce the adverse effects on a boat's crew.

- **The awareness of other water users, including the possible effects of wash.** A boat should be driven in such a way that it does not affect other boaters/water users. Reducing the wash produced when under way will contribute to this.

■ **The controls and the effect of current/tidal stream on the craft.** The helm should be fully aware of the effect that the controls have on the boat. In addition, that awareness should extend to the water that the boat is sitting in, as in a coastal situation this water may be moving.

■ **Boat handling at planing speeds, the use of trim tabs and/or power trim on an outboard/outdrive.** Most sportsboats can travel easily at high speed. The helm should be familiar with the handling characteristics of their boat while travelling at speed. These characteristics can be modified by various different trim angles of the engine/trim tabs.

■ **Planing boats only: The effects of propeller angle and its immersion, use of shallow drive and its drawbacks, planing and displacement speed handling, the differences between tiller and remote (console) steering and controls.** Outboard engines often allow for changing the trim of the engine. This can have a positive effect while under way in reducing drag and improving performance. The engine can often be tilted up to allow the boat to be operated in shallow water. The propeller will lose efficiency and there is a danger of sucking in debris from the bottom into the engine. The hull could also make contact with the ground. Care should be taken in these circumstances. Tiller steering does away with a steering wheel and remote gear lever/throttle. Instead, all these controls are found attached directly to the engine. The advantage is that they are simpler to control and cheaper. The disadvantage is that they can only be operated from the very rear of the craft.

■ **Oversight of untrained/inexperienced helms:** Discuss with students the safety precautions to be taken before offering a friend the opportunity to have a go at helming, including: what the kill cord does, and how to wear it; the controls; how and when to do a 'life saver' shoulder check; communicating changes of speed or direction; making smooth changes in direction – in an arc instead of sharp ones.

■ **Operating powerboats safely in a group:** When riding in a group, it is easy to become distracted just at a time when there is a lot going on. Keep safety front of mind by focusing on the following: keep a very good all-round lookout using effective 'life saver' shoulder checks; bear in mind that things which approach from behind are easy to miss; be sure to keep well clear of the stern of fast manoeuvrable vessels when jumping wake.

RYA Tender Operator Course

Aim: To teach tender driving up to the standard required to carry passengers and other crew members to and from the mother ship by day and night.

This course is designed to build on basic knowledge of powerboating and candidates should gain confidence in their own competence. They will have plenty of time for practising techniques for working with crew members and when short-handed. It is important that candidates understand that the emphasis of the course is on ship-to-shore transfers and associated skills, rather than coastal cruising.

Candidates should gain an appreciation of their role and responsibilities a as tender skipper in addition to helming skillfully and safely.

The course will be taught by an RYA Advanced Powerboat Instructor at an RYA-recognised centre. The award is not commercially endorsable.

The student to Instructor ratio should not exceed 3:1.

Practical

Preparation for Sea

Can:

Prepare the vessel, including:

- **Navigation equipment.** This initial session should cover checking navigation equipment set-up, such as which GPS datum it is referring to and understanding whether the depth is reading from the water surface or is offset to the keel. As most chart plotters have similar features, there's no need to become too concerned with the detail of a particular unit. It's a case of the candidates understanding the requirement to become familiar with the equipment on the vessel they will be skippering – examining the basic functions, knowing what data is available through changing the screens, how to alter the backlighting, etc.
- Bilge pump and alarms. Discuss the advantages/disadvantages of manual/automatic bilge pumps and those with a battery override.
- Essential safety equipment. Where is the equipment stowed? How and under what circumstances is it deployed?
- Stowage of warps and securing gear. Emphasise the importance of a tidy tender with regards to the safety of the vessel and those aboard.

Pre-departure Procedures

Understands:

- **Drive systems.** The types of drives commonly in use for tenders include outboards, inboard diesel, and jet drive. The pre-start checks for the particular vessel being used for training should be taught, with the students aware that they should learn the corresponding pre-start checks for the tenders they will be operating.
- **Emergency shutdown procedures for the vessel being used for training.**
- **The need for familiarity with procedures for refuelling onboard and at sea.** There are risks, hazards and precautions associated with this, plus an environmental impact. Candidates should ensure they are trained on this as part of their familiarisation with a new yacht.
- **Communication protocol with mother ship.** Each vessel will have a protocol for how often the tender operator contacts the mother ship. This may be at regular intervals or could depend upon the nature of the transfer, the conditions, and whether it is day or night.

Can:

- **Carry out fuel and mechanical checks on the vessel being used for training, including engines, cooling and lubrication systems.**
- **Safely start and shutdown engines.**
- **Diagnose basic engine-start problems.** Teach candidates a routine to diagnose basic starting issues. This may be worked methodically from 'console to engine', or may be broken into the three areas for faults: electrical, fuel, and mechanical.
- **Check fuel levels.** Candidates should know the location of fuel tap/shut-offs, and fuel filter sight glass.

Life Saving Apparatus (LSA)

Knowledge of:

- **Sources of information on different types of LSA.**

Understands:

- **The importance of familiarisation with the use of different types of LSA.** Students should know what LSAs are carried on a tender and how to deploy them.

Can:

- **Demonstrate the use of all LSA carried onboard.** Candidates should have an understanding of what each of the following items does and how it works: killcord; lifejackets; flares, and liferaft. They should understand where they can find information for the items on the tender they will be operating.

Lifejackets should be discussed in depth. Wearing a lifejacket in an open powerboat is prudent and professional. Consider what message your attitude to this piece of equipment gives off. Remember that it will be difficult for a skipper to convince passengers to put a lifejacket on if they themselves are not wearing one. Lifejackets nowadays are much more sleek, comfortable and smart-looking than previously. Lifejackets supplied for use at night should have a light, as this will probably be the only way of spotting a man overboard during the hours of darkness.

Killcord usage should be discussed and enforced rigorously throughout the course. It is an essential piece of safety equipment.

Boat Handling

Understands:

- The importance of having crew to assist in berthing operations.
- The importance of boat control in waves and adequate seating to minimise the possibility of injury.
- How to select an anchorage with due regard for the safety of the vessel and passengers who may be partaking in watersports.
- Towing water toys and the need for a spotter.
- **Tidal considerations.** Students should understand the effect tide has on ride comfort, and the ramifications for watersports, berthing and anchoring.

Can:

- Demonstrate the correct use of the killcord at all times when under way.
- Demonstrate berthing and docking skills in the following situations: beam to, bow to, and stern to, carried out with a crew member and short-handed.
- Helm considerately at planing speed.
- Recover an MOB by day and night.
- Anchor the vessel safely.

The boat-handling section is aimed at polishing the candidate's existing skills and helping them to manoeuvre smoothly with regard to their surroundings and the prevailing conditions. When practising berthing techniques, adequate time should be set aside for candidates to have experience of a variety of methods, e.g. using springs. They should gain confidence in their ability to helm the vessel smoothly. Practical activity can be punctuated with discussions on passenger safety and comfort, as well as considering how to transfer those with reduced mobility or restrictive clothing.

Rules of the Road

Knowledge of:

- **Sources of local bylaws.** The majority of this course should be taught practically, infusing theoretical knowledge into the practical training wherever possible. When discussing local bylaws under the 'Rules of the Road' section it would be useful to have laminated copies of some sample documents or to have them on a tablet so that they can be discussed during the course. The aim is to bring the subject to life. Ignoring local bylaws can have serious consequences. For example, speeding in France carries a maximum six-month prison sentence and the possibility of being banned from French territorial waters for five years.

Some resources are available from the RYA Training Department. Keep your eyes open and pick up anything useful from local harbourmasters' offices to supplement your resources.

Understands:

- **The importance of adhering to local bylaws.**

Can:

- **Apply the International Regulations for the Prevention of Collisions at Sea (IRPCS).** The emphasis is on a practical working knowledge of the IRPCS. Focus on concepts and practical application, and be opportunistic when afloat. Lights should be at a basic level – for example, identifying that there is a vessel and whether it is moving or at anchor.
- **Demonstrate a good sense of situational awareness, including the ability to conduct dynamic risk assessment given the prevailing conditions and location.**

Passenger Safety and Comfort

Knowledge of:

- **Sources of information regarding maximum number of people and payload.** Take a look at the manufacturer's plate.

Understands:

- **When to instruct passengers to wear appropriate LSA.**
- **The importance of boat control in waves and appropriate seating to minimise the possibility of injury or ejection.**
- **The requirement to comply with the maximum number of people and payload.**
- **The hazards associated with non-compliant passengers and those under the influence of alcohol.**
- **The hazards associated with less-mobile passengers and children.**

- Strategies for ensuring the safety of non-English speaking passengers.
- The importance of selecting a safe place to meet and greet passengers.
- The need to pre-plan onward land transportation of passengers.

There are scenarios for use in prompting discussion among the candidates on the topic of dealing with people. These can be used to add context and variety during the practical boat-handling exercises.

Can:

- Brief the crew on passage plan, and roles and responsibilities.
- Give an effective passenger-safety briefing.
- **Give an effective demonstration of all relevant LSA and location.** Candidates need to be able to deliver a smooth, confident and informative passenger briefing. Think about the safety briefing given on a plane. A briefing should contain an introduction; who is in charge; information on the need for passengers to remain seated (and possibly holding on); how to tell the crew if you are uncomfortable or wish the boat to slow down; how to put on a lifejacket (including recommendations regarding wearing one for the transfer); what to do in an emergency; expected conditions and duration of transfer.
- Embark and disembark passengers safely.
- Drive appropriate to prevailing weather and sea conditions, with due consideration to keeping all onboard comfortable and dry.

Daytime Pilotage

Understands:

- **The benefit of agreeing and lodging the pilotage plan with the Master or Officer of the Watch (OOW).** This course covers monitoring and executing a plan. Tender operators should seek guidance from the OOW regarding their intended ship-to-shore plan.
- **The requirement for a safety margin when using chart plotters and other electronic navigation aids.**
- **The need to use a secondary means of position fixing when using electronic navigation aids, including the use of verifiable waypoints.** There are many factors which can affect the accuracy of a GPS-derived position, from atmospheric conditions or a GPS jammer nearby to poor electrical connection or the speed of the screen update. Candidates should learn to identify verifiable waypoints which, given the rate of screen update, they will identify as having reached prior to the chart plotter announcing their arrival at a waypoint.
- Considerations for local environmental conditions, hazards and other water users.
- The importance of maintaining contact with the mother vessel at all times.
- Safe speed for navigation.

Can:

- **Produce an effective daytime pilotage plan.** A simple plan allows for short ship-to-shore transfers (approximately 1–2 nautical miles). Remember that tender operators are unlikely to have a chart on board, so a sketch pilotage plan would be useful as an aide memoire for spotting their waypoints.
- **Use charts and publications.** This is for the purpose of geographical context and refamiliarisation. Most of the planning will take place directly on the chart plotter.
- **Interpret lateral and cardinal buoyage systems A and B.**
- **Use a chart plotter for navigation afloat.**
- **Use waypoint navigation.** When inputting a basic plan, consider it in three stages:
1.   On a large scale, drop in two waypoints A–B (mother ship to port entrance).
2.   Zoom in and follow the line. Does it put the boat close to any hazards or restricted areas? If it does, drop in a waypoint and move it well clear of the hazard. Repeat this as many times as is necessary to have a safe route.
3.   Zoom in on each waypoint. Is it verifiable by sight? For example, is there a landmark or buoyage that can be referred to? Teach the candidates not to rely on the waypoint alarm to alert them that they have arrived, as they will already have passed their waypoint. It should be considered a back up.
- **Use pilotage to enter a port by day.**

Night-time Pilotage

Understands:

- **The additional hazards associated with moving passengers by water during the hours of darkness.**

Can:

- Take charge of a power-driven vessel during the hours of darkness, including but not limited to short passages between harbour and mother vessel.
- Produce an effective night-time pilotage plan.
- Demonstrate ability to keep a proper lookout by all available means.
- Identify position at all times.

The night-pilotage exercise is a very basic one. The exercise should imitate the kind of pilotage that tender operators may make when transporting guests between a quayside or waterside restaurant and the mother ship. It is not intended to be an Advanced Powerboat-level exercise. They are not required to find unlit positions or to undertake complex navigation. The aim is to experience boating at night, and gain a realisation of the hazards and an appreciation that a simple plan should be made and followed. An example might be to identify a nearby bay which can be where the imaginary yacht is at anchor. For the plan to be successful the candidate would need to be able to follow it singlehandedly. Think about how to make it simple enough so that the candidate can identify their waypoints to change course by sight, for example when this or that is abeam, or when the aerial on the cliff lines up with the fixed red on the entrance to the port.

Emergency Situations

Knowledge of:

- Helicopter rescue procedures.
- Local safe havens/points of refuge.

Understands:

- Effective management of an emergency situation by day and at night.
- The importance of keeping an up-to-date head count of all persons on board.
- Fire prevention and fighting.
- The action to take in the event of hull damage/loss of watertight integrity.
- What to do in a medical emergency.
- The principles of towing and being towed.
- The danger of cold shock.

Can:

- Simulate a distress alert by all available means.

The emergency section should cover how to raise the alarm; finding out about the emergency services in the operating area, and the importance of an Emergency Action Plan (EAP).

Theory

Types of Tender

Knowledge of:

- Different types of tender.
- Different types of propulsion systems: outdrive, outboard, jet drive, forward-facing drives, shaft drive.

Understands:

- **The handling characteristics for various types of common hull forms.** In addition to discussing what different hull types are best suited to, take time to discuss what happens when they are used for other purposes, e.g. a particular boat may be great for producing good wake for towed sports, but the trim angle required may impact on field of vision going forward and thus objects in the water may be more difficult to spot.

Launch and Recovery

Knowledge of:

- Various methods of launch and recovery from the mother vessel while at anchor and stopped in the water.

Understands:

- **The requirement to gain onboard type-specific training.** This is not a practical session as training is bespoke to each system and forms part of the safety management onboard each yacht. This section is to be covered very briefly; the candidates should come away with the strong message that they must undertake specific training on the systems used on the yacht they are working on.

Legislation and Guidance

Knowledge of:

- **The requirement to maintain a current MCA (Yacht) Officer of the Watch Training Record Book.** For those working in the Deck Department of a yacht and wishing to progress up through the UK Maritime & Coastguard Agency (MCA) Yacht Deck qualifications, the MCA requires the completion of a '(Yacht) Officer of the Watch Training Record Book' as part of the prerequisites towards the (UK) MCA OOW (Y) 3000gt Certificate of Competence.

  The International Convention on Standards of Training, Certification and Watchkeeping for Seafarers 1978, as amended, regulates the training and competence of seafarers internationally. The MCA regulates the training and certification of seafarers working in

UK-registered yachts in line with the requirements of STCW95. As part of this training, every candidate for certification as Officer of the Watch (Yachts, less than 3000gt) must complete an approved training programme which is structured to assist an officer candidate achieve the necessary standard of competence.

The OOW(Y) training programme is a combination of shorebased education and training, and onboard service. The (Yacht) OOW Training Record Book is an integral part of this training programme and should be completed during periods of onboard service. The (Yacht) OOW Training Record Book not only allows for the practical assessment of assignments but also provides a comprehensive record of shorebased training and onboard service. The MCA favours the (Yacht) OOW Training Record Book being completed over a three-year period, in line with the 36 months of yacht service required for entry to the OOW training programme for those new to yachting, and a minimum of a 12-month period if you have further prior experience.

The book must be fully completed, with the Master or a duly authorised officer verifying that the various 'assignments' and 'tasks' are complete by signing the appropriate sections.

- **The RYA Code of Practice for safe watersports operations.**
- **RYA guidance on small high-speed craft passenger safety.**

Understands:

- **The importance of carrying the correct documents.** Tenders should be marked T/T [name of the mother ship]. If the tender's use extends beyond ship-to-shore transport, some jurisdictions may treat the tender as a pleasure craft in its own right and the registration requirement and other rules outlined here may apply to the tender independently of the mother ship. If the owner of the vessel is not onboard, in some countries the skipper will need a letter authorising use of the vessel to ensure the loan is not seen as illegal chartering.

There is a core set of paperwork (your ship's papers) which, together with your passport, any other personal paperwork and any country-specific documentation or publications you may be required to carry on board, should enable you to satisfy a foreign customs official, if required.

Ship's Papers: Registration document; ship's radio licence; insurance; VAT status.

Personal Papers: Passport; evidence of competence; proof of authority to operate maritime radio.

Vessel-specific Training

Knowledge of:

- Additional regulated training available: RYA Intermediate Powerboat; RYA Advanced Powerboat; RYA/MCA Advanced Powerboat Certificate of Competence; MCA Fast Rescue Craft.

Understands:

- The importance of vessel- and equipment-specific training.

Candidates should understand that this course is an introduction to tender operations and that there is more for them to learn once they work onboard a yacht. They should assimilate the knowledge and experience gained on the course with the onboard training they should receive prior to using any specialist equipment.

RYA Intermediate Powerboat Day Cruising Course

Aim: To provide students with the knowledge and skills to be able safely and successfully to undertake and complete a short coastal passage by day.

It is expected that candidates should be competent to the level of RYA Powerboat Level 2.

It is strongly recommended that candidates hold an appropriate first aid certificate and also a VHF operator's licence. Candidates must be a minimum age of 16 years old.

The course is run over two days and contains enhanced levels of theory and practical skills to prepare the students for longer passages and the extra planning that this will entail. The theory within the course will support the practical elements, which will make up the greater proportion of the course.

The theory knowledge required of the student is recommended to be that of the level of RYA Day Skipper (Theory).

Students will use the theory skills taught during the course to create a passage plan, which they will then execute. The plan will use both traditional and electronic navigation techniques.

The course will be taught by an RYA Advanced Powerboat Instructor at an RYA-recognised centre. The award is not commercially endorsable.

The student to Instructor ratio should not exceed 3:1.

Practical

The practical skills taught on the Intermediate course are not fundamentally different from those found in the RYA Powerboat Level 2 course.

Therefore, the Instructor may revisit some or all Level 2 skills to ensure that the student can perform them in what may be more challenging conditions or venues.

The main differences are likely to be:

- They may be taught in a different and possibly larger boat to that used for the Level 2.
- The Instructor may expect greater accuracy for some skills.
- The Instructor will expect consistency in performing skills.
- The Instructor may ask the students to perform the skills in a stronger tideway.
- The Instructor may ask the students to perform the skills in stronger winds.
- A combination of the above two factors may produce rougher water than the student may have experienced in the past.

Specific Practical Skills for the Intermediate Award

- Demonstrate an awareness of wind and tide.
- Moor alongside in a marina berth.
- Demonstrate a practical application of techniques for pilotage in local waters.
- Apply the techniques learnt in the theory sessions and successfully complete a practical passage.
- Fix position using traditional and electronic means.
- Pick up a man overboard (dummy).
- Know how and when to raise the alarm.

If undertaking a passage in more open water, the students should be able to trim the boat and engine according to the conditions. This will produce a more comfortable ride for the occupants and the boat should achieve optimum performance. All boats differ, so how much trim and when to use it should be practised on the course, preferably in calmer waters, so that the student is familiar with the concept. This will be required when undertaking the open-water passage.

Trimming for Rougher Conditions

Upwind Driving

As the boat will be driving up and over the waves, to prevent the bow from rising too high on the wave crest, the engine should be trimmed further in/down.

Downwind Driving

To help increase visibility and help prevent the bow from 'burying' in a trough, trim the engine further out/up.

Theory

As the purpose of the course is to teach students to complete a short coastal passage by day, the Instructor should teach the students a variety of navigational techniques not covered in the RYA Powerboat Level 2 syllabus.

Section A Theory

Knowledge of:

- **Use of marina locks.** These will vary in their use and information on how to use them correctly should be obtained from the marina or lock-keeper before using them.

Understands:

- **Latitude and longitude.** The theoretical vertical and horizontal grid lines that surround the earth and are used to 'fix' positions. Lines of longitude are 'great circles' that surround the earth pole to pole with the zero meridian passing through Greenwich, London. Lines of latitude are the lines running parallel from the equator upwards and downwards to the poles.

- **The principles of GPS and chart plotters.** There are numerous global navigation satellite systems, such as GPS and GLONASS. GNSS uses a constellation of a least 24 satellites that orbit the earth and offer an electronic position fix. A GNSS unit is a relatively simple device offering limited navigational information. Chart plotters give an electronic 'chart' picture on a screen with an overlaid position of the vessel from a GNSS receiver. Both are very useful but have some drawbacks that the Instructor should rbing to the attention of the students.

- **Sources of forecast information and the interpretation of forecasts.** There are various agencies issuing weather forecasts for marine use. Instructors should inform students which ones offer the most useful information to the small-boat user. Interpretation should include wind strength and how it is given, direction and the effect on sea state, precipitation, and temperature.

- **Tidal heights at secondary ports.** Nautical almanacs give limited information about secondary ports. Information on how to expand on this information for all times of tides should be explained using simple diagrams.

- **How to use a plotting instrument and plot a course to steer.** There are various devices available to measure bearings on a chart accurately. Students should become familiar with their use to be able to measure and record bearings when plotting a course (including magnetic variation).

- **How to issue distress by various means.** In practice, this will include the different types of flares available, how to deploy them and their limitations. Use of VHF marine radio with DSC capability should also be covered, including giving a Mayday call.

Can:

- **Work out tidal heights for standard ports using a tidal curve.** Students should know the height of the tide for any given time of its range. This can be calculated by using a tidal curve for the standard port nearest to where the school is operating. Once calculated on the curve, this information can be used in conjunction with the chart of the area to calculate heights of tide over features and can be taken afloat to refer to during the passage.

- **Use true and magnetic bearings.** When 'working up' a course to steer, students should be aware of the difference between the true bearing given on a chart and the magnetic bearing that will be used when following a compass.

- **Bearing and distance.** In creating a passage plan, the direction from one point to another will be given in a 'compass bearing', using north as a reference point. The distance from one such point to another can also be measured using the latitude scale on the side of the chart.

- **Interpret chart symbols.** The nautical chart has numerous symbols to represent features found on it. Knowing them all would be difficult, so knowing how to use Admiralty publication 5011 Symbols and Abbreviations Used on Admiralty Charts is recommended.

- **Interpret tidal diamonds and tidal streams.** Among the symbols found on a nautical chart are tidal diamonds. These are locations of where tidal data has been recorded. This data is given in an abridged form on the chart in a table. It gives the speed and the direction of the stream at that location at hourly increments either side of high water at a nearby standard port.

- **Use of pilot books.** These publications give a wealth of extra knowledge about specific areas not necessarily shown on the chart. They contain photographs, enlarged chart extracts and useful local information about ports, harbours and creeks.

- **Interpret lateral and cardinal buoyage.** Although these buoys are positioned primarily for large, commercial shipping in busy areas, the leisure boater can make good use of them when conducting a passage. Knowing what they are, what they represent and how to use them safely is essential.

- **Implement IRPCS, particularly rules 5, 6, 7, 8, 9, 12–19, and 23.** The regulations apply to smaller craft as well as larger ones and students need to know their meaning and application when they are operating their craft. Students should be familiar with the rules as applied, but don't need to know the rule numbers and content off by heart.

- **Use GPS waypoint navigation.** Just as students need to be able to plot a course between positions on a paper chart, the equivalent positions on an electronic chart are known as waypoints. Electronic navigation involves using XTE (cross-track error), SOG (speed over ground), COG (course over ground), BTW (bearing to waypoint) and DTW (distance to waypoint), all functions built into GPS devices.

- **Use a laminated chart afloat.** Once a course has been plotted on a paper chart, it can be transferred onto a more durable plasticised one. This can then be used to navigate once afloat.

- **Use pilotage to enter an unfamiliar port by day.** This is the end result of all the work and calculations done in the classroom. Students should have a workable plan that will allow them to take their craft safely into an area of which they have no practical knowledge.

- All of the above should ensure that the student can **navigate** when required using all the resources and techniques described above.

Top Tips

- When 'working-up' a passage plan, students should be encouraged to create their own shorthand chart containing all their necessary navigation information. They can then follow this as a guide while afloat without the need to refer to a large, unwieldy paper chart.

RYA Advanced Powerboat Day & Night Course

Aim: The course is designed to teach boat-handling, seamanship, pilotage and navigation up to the standards that are required to drive a planing powerboat safely by day and night in tidal coastal waters with which the candidate may be familiar.

The boats used can be planing or displacement ones that carry and display the correct lights that conform to IRPCS.

Students (and instructors) must wear a minimum 150 Newton lifejacket with MCA-approved light for the night exercise.

Students should be competent to the standard of the RYA Intermediate Powerboat Certificate and have a thorough knowledge of navigation and chartwork to the standard of Coastal Skipper/RYA Yachtmaster Shorebased Certificate. It is strongly recommended that candidates hold a valid first aid certificate and VHF operator's certificate.

The course duration will be two days with a night exercise. It will be taught by an RYA Advanced Instructor. Students must be 17 years old or over.

The student to Instructor ratio should not exceed 3:1.

Practical

Preparation for Sea

- **Prepare the powerboat.** Students should ensure that the boat has all the necessary equipment and safety equipment for putting to sea safely. Requirements for operating at night will need to be taken into consideration. The correct light configuration will need to be displayed as well as lamps and/or head torches for the crew. Instrument lights and chart plotter illumination must also be functioning correctly. In addition to the usual equipment, boats must also have fitted a correctly functioning log and echo sounder.
- **Carry out fuel and engine checks.** Routine checks should be made, including fuel filters.
- **Stow and secure gear.** Equipment must be safely stowed to prevent it moving while under way. All crew must know the whereabouts of all kit, especially the safety/emergency equipment.

Boat Handling

Knowledge of:

- **Differences for a twin-engine vessel.** Twin-engine installations allow for greater manoeuvrability, especially in confined spaces. While running one engine ahead and the other astern, the pivot point moves more centrally in the boat, and it will turn in its own length.

Understands:

- **The importance of boat control in waves and adequate seating to minimise the possibility of injury or ejection.** The Advanced award will mean operating in potentially more challenging conditions to those previously experienced.

- Upwind driving. As the boat powers up and over the waves, the engine should be throttled back as the bow pushes over the crest. This will cause the bow to drop and power should be applied again to raise the bow for the next trough. If possible, the engine should be trimmed in/down. Driving upwind demands skill from the helm to read the wave pattern and use the throttle to keep the hull of the boat in the water while using sufficient power to push up and through wave crests.

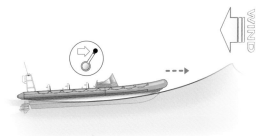

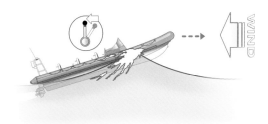

- Downwind driving. To help increase visibility and to help prevent the bow from 'burying' in a trough, the boat should be driven up the back of the largest wave in the vicinity. The bow should be pointing 'uphill'. The helm then holds the boat in this position and takes care not to overtake the wave and drop into the trough ahead. Eventually, the wave will crumble and dissipate and the helm can power on and look for the next large wave. If possible, the engine should be trimmed up/out. Careful driving will improve the comfort and safety of the crew.

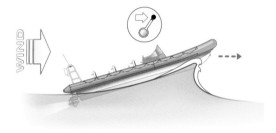

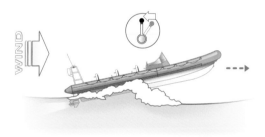

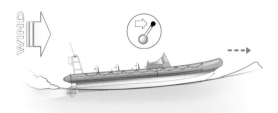

- **Characteristics of various hull forms and propeller configurations.** There are numerous hull types that can be used successfully at sea. Which hull is chosen will generally depend on the use of the craft.
- **Action to be taken in rough water** – see above.

Can:

■ **Demonstrate a practical understanding and correct use of power trim and trim tabs.**
Trim tabs are found on the outer edges of the transom of larger, planing craft, usually with propeller shafts where the propellers can be individually trimmed. They can be used together to trim the bow up or down for adverse sea conditions. They can also be used independently if running in a cross sea to balance the hull in an upright attitude.

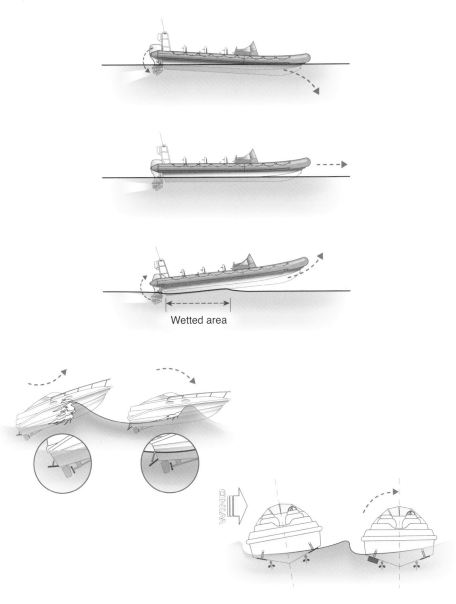

Wetted area

■ **Demonstrate an awareness of the effects of wind and tide when manoeuvring including:**

 ▪ Steering to transits and in buoyed channels. To counter the effects of a tidal stream running across the course a craft is making, transits can be used to ensure that the correct course is held. These could be observed either ahead or astern. They may be charted, known transits, leading marks, or could be improvised while on passage.

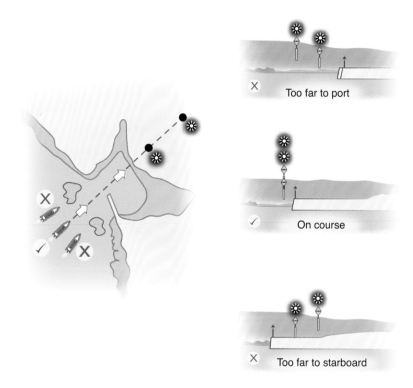

Too far to port

On course

Too far to starboard

 ▪ Turning in a confined space. When carrying out this manoeuvre, wind and tide can assist or interfere with the turning of the craft. As a general rule, a manoeuvre made into wind/tide can be extended slightly longer than one made with the wind/tide.

 ▪ Berthing in various wind/tide conditions (see RYA Powerboat Level 2 section).

 ▪ Picking up and leaving a mooring buoy (see RYA Powerboat Level 2 section).

■ Demonstrate the correct length of killcord at all times. Using the killcord supplied by the manufacturer will ensure that this condition is adhered to.

■ Pick up a man overboard in various conditions. The Advanced course may allow the MOB drill to take place in more challenging conditions. The Instructor may instigate the drill at any stage during the course, including the night passage.

Passage Making and Responsibilities as Skipper

Understands:

- **The importance of pre-trip planning.** Prior to any passage at sea, the skipper should make a plan of what is to be undertaken. This should be recorded in such a way that it can be referred to while afloat.

- **Planning and making coastal passages, taking into account the relevant navigational hazards, the type of boat and strengths of the crew.** As above.

- **Chart plotters and radar, their advantages and limitations.** Both instruments have many benefits and can enhance navigation under way in craft. However, they are prone to 'operator error', so the helm and crew should be fully familiar with their operation. This is best practised before they are needed on passage. Both units are best operated by crew members, leaving the helm to concentrate on driving the boat without distractions.

Can:

- **Organise the navigation, safety and welfare of the crew during a passage.** The skipper of the craft becomes the 'manager' and should have considered and be aware of all the elements on board. Crew and their tasks should be monitored while on passage.

- **Navigate at higher speed using a range of techniques.** Prior planning will help to ensure that a sound passage plan is created before embarking. The skipper should not rely on one technique or instrument only. By having several, should one fail or not be as accurate as expected, the back-up can be used without disruption.

- **Use electronic navigational equipment for planning and undertaking a passage, including the use of waypoints, routes and XTE, SOG, COG, BTW, DTW** (See Intermediate award). As well as planning the passage using traditional techniques, the skipper should be able to utilise electronic navigation equipment that is readily available.

Pilotage

Can:

◾ **Carry out pilotage plans and pilotage for entry into or departure from a harbour.** In creating a passage plan, pilotage details for harbours or creeks can be taken from the chart of the area and the pilot book. The craft can then be brought safely into the haven using the navigation buoys and marks laid out in that area. Prior knowledge of what to expect and look for will ease the task of the navigator.

◾ **Use leading and clearing lines, transits, back bearings and soundings as aids to pilotage:**

▪ Leading lines. A line chosen on the chart to a known object. It is used to keep the craft clear of a hazard close to the object.

▪ Transits. Using two fixed objects or features to keep the craft on the intended track. They can be charted, but if the area is familiar they can be improvised.

▪ Back bearing. A surprisingly accurate but little-used form of navigation used to keep a craft on track, usually, but not restricted to, leaving a harbour.

▪ Soundings. The echo sounder is perhaps the simplest electronic navigational device. However, it is very accurate. It can be used when approaching land/harbour to check progress, or can be used to run along a known (and pre-checked) contour line to approach a feature safely.

Leading lines

Back bearing

Craft zig-zags along the depth contour to enter the harbour in poor visibility

Soundings

Theory

Meteorology

Understands:

- **Terms used in shipping forecasts, including Beaufort Scale, and their significance to small craft.** Marine forecasts use terms not normally given on general weather forecasts for the non-boater. Wind strengths and their associated sea state should be familiar to the students.

- **Sources of forecast information and interpretation of forecasts including synoptic charts.** Before putting to sea, a comprehensive awareness of the current situation and developing weather should be gained. This will include using various sources of weather including the inshore waters forecast with particular reference to wind strength and direction. The significance of high- and low-pressure systems, isobars and their meaning, warm, cold and occluded fronts and the passage of weather systems should all be understood.

- **The significance of meteorological trends.** By using a variety and combination of weather sources and forecasts, weather patterns and trends can be recognised in advance, enabling better-informed plans to be made for forthcoming passages.

Can:

- **Interpret a synoptic chart.** Synoptic charts offer valuable extra information that is not always gained from more readily available sources of weather information. The combination of isobars, readily identified weather systems, high- and low-pressure areas, warm, cold and occluded fronts, troughs and ridges will give those who have an understanding of these symbols the ability to make much more accurate predictions of what is in store over a period of time and be much more able to recognise trends.

- **Use and interpret forecasts to make decisions about passages.** All of the above.

Rules of the Road

Can:

- **Apply the IRPCS.** The regulations apply to smaller craft as well as larger ones and students need to know their meaning and application when they are operating their own. This is particularly important during the hours of darkness, so students should be familiar with the light characteristics of vessels they are likely to encounter on passage at night, as well as day shapes for daylight hours.

Use of Engines

Knowledge of:

- **How to change a propeller.** The splined hubs on modern propellers are all but universal, but there may be differences in various manufacturers. Students should be familiar with the removal and fitting procedure required.

- **Propeller pitch and diameter.** Engines are generally supplied with the correct propeller for the engine's power output. There is some flexibility in the recommended propeller, so students should be aware of the various options available for different applications.

- **Propeller ventilation and cavitation:**
  - *Ventilation* – this condition occurs when air attaches itself to the blades of a spinning propeller, which causes it to lose 'grip' on the water. It becomes apparent to the operator when the engine 'over-revs' and loses drive. It can be easily cured by throttling back to idle or neutral to allow the air bubbles to clear away. It is often caused when an engine is trimmed up/out for optimum performance and the helm performs a turn, causing the propeller to rise closer to the surface of the water.
  - *Cavitation* – this is where water boils on the surface of the propeller blades, causing minute air bubbles. Over time, these will cause localised damage to the blades that will eventually require the propeller to be replaced.

Understands:

- **Checks to be made before starting, during running and after stopping for diesel and petrol engines.** Prior to starting any engine, the oil level should be checked, usually with a simple dipstick. The level and condition of the oil should be noted and if there are adverse visual signs, remedial action taken. If a petrol engine is installed in an engine compartment the vapour from the fuel can accumulate, so the engine space should be fully ventilated before starting. Blowers should be fitted to carry out this function. Diesel engines may require 'pre-warming' before starting. If the engine is an inboard unit, then seacocks that allow cooling water to be taken in should be opened after the filters have been checked and cleaned. Fresh water for the heat exchanger should also be checked and topped up if necessary. Once started, all engines whether inboard or outboard should have checks performed to ensure that the cooling water is being drawn in and passed around the cooling system. On outboard engines there will be a purpose-built 'telltale' jet. On inboard engines the cooling water is often ejected through the exhaust. Temperature gauges will need to be monitored regularly during running. Close-down procedures are often the reverse of the start-up routine. Outboard engines will benefit from a flush through with fresh water.

■ **Periodic checks on engines, electrical systems and spark plugs, water filters and pump impellors.** Modern outboard engines have very few 'user maintenance' items and, providing that they are regularly serviced to the manufacturer's recommended intervals, they will provide trusted service. However, a fuel filter that can be inspected and drained if the fuel shows signs of contamination is a wise precaution. Inboard engines allow for more regular routine checks. Belts, pulleys, lubrication points, mountings and filters can all be easily accessed and checked.

■ **Spares.** Outboard engines now have few spare parts that can be fitted by the average owner/operator. New spark plugs, correctly gapped, may be useful to carry, as would the correct spare fuses. A spare propeller might also make a useful addition to the inventory as well as the correct tools required to fit it. Inboard engine spares might include an impellor, pulley belt, filter and the necessary tools to bleed the diesel fuel system.

Emergency Situations

Correct action to take in an emergency situation. The following scenarios each require the appropriate action in order to contain the situation and ensure the safety of all personnel on board:

■ **Fire prevention and fighting.** Petrol engines present a higher potential risk than diesel. However, sensible action such as care while refueling, siting fuel tanks in appropriate locations, and carrying out regular checks on fuel lines and connections will reduce the risk of a mishap. Fighting fires must be undertaken with caution and the correct extinguisher for the fuel type must be carried.

■ **Hull damage/watertight integrity.** Caring for the vessel and not allowing the hull to be damaged will prevent a serious situation. Allowing the vessel repeatedly to take to the ground will weaken the hull and cause water ingress. Collision with another craft, debris or the ground will also have serious consequences. Few craft carry equipment to deal specifically with this occurrence, so improvisation will be required. Soft wood bungs and a mallet will be effective if there is a small breach to the hull, but taking the vessel into shallow water to take to the ground will help prevent total loss.

■ **What to do in a medical emergency.** If the emergency requires more treatment than is provided by a simple first aid kit, then a call to the emergency services (Coastguard) is likely. A 'Mayday' or 'Pan Pan' call (depending on the severity of the situation) must be considered and it may require the casualty to be evacuated. These agencies are professionals and are well used to dealing with this type of emergency and will be in a far better position to make recommendations than a boat crew, so they should not feel intimidated in making the call.

■ **Towing and being towed.** Simple breakdowns can often be dealt with by the offer of a friendly tow to a safe haven. Before doing so, the strong points on the towing vessel should be prepared, as should the warps. The towed vessel normally uses its painter, but other strong points should be considered, e.g. a Samson post, or other strong fittings.

- **Helicopter rescue procedures.** If a helicopter is deployed to a craft, its crew will direct operations once on scene. They may communicate via VHF prior to arrival, as once overhead, verbal communication is impossible. If there is a breeze, the craft is asked to lie ahull, and the helicopter is most likely to drop a 'highline' into the craft. It will then back away to a high hover and the winchperson will be lowered down. The crew on the craft will be encouraged to pull on the highline to draw the winchperson into the craft. There are two points to note. **Never** attach the highline to any part of the craft, and crew shouldn't touch the winchperson until they have 'earthed' themself before boarding. The new generation of aircraft does not generate as much static electricity as the older Sea Kings, though. Once onboard, the winchperson will instruct the crew what is required.

- **Issuing distress by all available means.** The most effective way to issue a distress signal is by VHF using DSC, but crews should be aware that they follow this with a voice message Mayday call. Flares would be considered the next most effective. Red parachute flares are the most visible, and then handheld red pinpoint flares are effective at indicating which vessel requires assistance. Mobile phones can be used, but they have limited range and, unlike VHF, they do not 'broadcast' their signal, so they are considered to be only of back-up use. Thereafter, visual signals to other vessels or to persons ashore can be used, but are considered to be less effective than those above.

- **Search patterns.** The most effective pattern for a lone craft is an expanding box. It puts less pressure on the crew in what is already a difficult situation if the search is for a 'real' MOB. If sight of the MOB is lost, it should be started immediately and a Mayday call should be made to the Coastguard at the same time so that they can use their own computer programmes to help with the search pattern. The sector search has been shown to be more accurate, but it demands more of the crew to carry it out correctly, which may be too difficult in a 'real' situation.

- **The danger of cold shock and hypothermia.** Cold shock is not treatable, but students should be aware of its effects should they find themselves overboard. The immediate effect is that of involuntary gasping for breath, which increases the heart rate. At this point, victims unaware of the situation can take in water, exacerbating their condition. The condition lasts for only a few minutes and, if the victim is aware of its effects, they should be able to have the presence of mind to remain calm while the symptoms subside. They can then take stock of their plight and prepare for rescue. If immersed for a long period, hypothermia is likely. The correct clothing, including a drysuit, can help delay the effects. Crew recovering a person from the water should be aware of the possibility of hypothermia and should take care in how the victim is brought onboard i.e. horizontally, if at all possible. They should then be kept in that position and insulated from the elements, but not warmed externally. They should be evacuated to hospital without delay.

Night Cruising

Can:

- **Take charge of a powerboat at night, including leaving and entering a harbour.** The skipper should be the 'manager' of the craft and crew. They should make best use of all the crew to operate the craft safely and effectively while on passage. This will mean allocating tasks to the crew so that all are involved. If an effective passage plan has been created, then entering and leaving a harbour will not present any difficulties, but rather will be part of a predetermined strategy.

- **Demonstrate ability at keeping a proper lookout and identifying lit and unlit positions at night.** As described above, a well-prepared plan will allow the skipper to find all proposed marks. Although they will be responsible for keeping a lookout, they will utilise their crew effectively to assist with this, so that the crew and craft are safe at all times.

Advanced Powerboat Examination: Notes for Examiners

Examiners

Examiners will be Powerboat Trainers or RYA Yachtmaster Examiners (Power) who have attended a briefing on the conduct of Advanced Powerboat Examinations and who have been registered by the RYA as Advanced Powerboat Examiners.

Authorisation of Exams

Candidates may book their exam online through the RYA website and an Examiner will be allocated to them by the RYA.

Alternatively, RYA Recognised -Training Centres can also book exams on behalf of their students by contacting Examiners directly but should use several different Examiners in rotation. A centre should not use an Examiner who is on its own staff or who has been involved in the student's training, unless in exceptional circumstances where no other Examiner is available and only with the prior approval of the RYA Chief Examiner. A list of Examiners is available from training@rya.org.uk.

Exam Fee

See the RYA website for details of the exam fee. Whether the exam is booked online or direct with the Examiner the candidate pays by credit/debit card or cheque to the Examiner PRIOR TO the start of the exam.

Examiners may not accept any payment from the candidates for expenses incurred in connection with an exam nor should they accept cash payments under any circumstances.

Candidate's Eligibility

Before the start of an exam, the Examiner must verify the candidate's claim to have the specified experience. If there is any doubt as to whether or not the necessary seatime has been completed the Examiner should point this out and the candidate given the opportunity to withdraw. If the exam is booked directly with the Examiner or allocated via the online booking system, the Examiner is advised to verify eligibility rather than waiting until the day of the exam.

Boat and Venue

For an own-boat exam, the candidate must provide a seaworthy boat and equipment complying with the requirements in the candidate's notes. The exam must be conducted at a coastal venue with sufficient lit and unlit marks to undertake the night exercise. If in any doubt please enquire with the RYA Chief Instructor, Power prior to agreeing to examine in an area with which you are unfamiliar.

The Exam

The exam will have three parts:

1. Classroom assessment and passage planning for night exercise

2. Boat handling in daylight

3. Night boat handling and navigation exercise.

The order that you run items 1 and 2 is up to you but don't run out of daylight whilst stuck in the classroom.

Section 1 of the exam involves an oral and chartwork planning test, which must be conducted at a table either in a room ashore or onboard a vessel with an enclosed chart table. Examiners should be using passage planning and navigation questions from the Coastal Skipper/RYA Yachtmaster Offshore Shorebased course or alternatively adapt their own theory exam as they see fit. It is not possible to take this part of the test in an open boat. The candidate will also need to plan the passage section which will need to be partly chart-based and also using electronic navigational techniques. You must include IRPCS and meteorology and a broad range of questions from across the entire syllabus. The level of theory knowledge expected of candidates recently changed from from Day Skipper to Coastal Skipper/RYA Yachtmaster Offshore Shorebased standard. Since 2013 all candidates presenting themselves for examination should be at Coastal Skipper theory level or above.

Section 2 is conducted aboard the vessel in daylight hours and will consist of safety brief, engine and craft checks, boat handling (as far as possible this should be conducted in a tidal stream), man overboard, pilotage by day, general seamanship and a variety of berthing manoeuvres.

For Section 3 the candidate should be asked to plan and undertake a night passage using lit and unlit marks. In some circumstances where the candidate is very familiar with the area, mostly unlit marks may be used. The Examiner may ask questions on IRPCS or other parts of the syllabus during the pilotage exercise but should avoid overloading the candidate during crucial points of the night passage.

It is perfectly acceptable to travel somewhere in section 2 in daylight and carry out section 3 as the return leg in darkness.

Conduct of the Examination

Examiners should follow the guidelines in the G20 RYA Powerboat Logbook for the standard of the Advanced Certificate.

There are two general principles, which should be taken as an overall guide:

1. It is the Examiner's task to give the candidate the opportunity to show competence in a powerboat.

2. At the end of the exam the candidate should feel, whatever the outcome, that they have had a full, fair and searching test.

Candidates should be made aware that they are responsible for the safety of the vessel and that they are considered to be 'in charge' during the time in which they are examined. They should not expect an Examiner to be stepping in to take avoiding action, although in reality an Examiner must be prepared to do this at times if he or she feels it is necessary.

Candidate Numbers and Duration of Exam

No more than three candidates may be examined in one session.

For one candidate	4–5 hours
For two candidates	5–6 hours
For three candidates	6–7 hours

If there is only one candidate they must bring a crew member to drive the vessel when the candidate is otherwise occupied.

Scenarios

As far as possible avoid role-playing or artificial exercises. It is better to ask the candidate what they would do in the event of, say engine failure, rather than devising role-playing games to demonstrate the same point. Where possible use 'real' navigational and tidal-calculation tasks to test the candidate's knowledge and ability rather than 'practice exercises'.

Stress Management

It is reasonable to expect the candidate to take charge of a powerboat even in quite difficult circumstances, but the pressure should come from the conditions and not from the Examiner.

Candidates react to the exam situation in a variety of ways and the Examiner must make an early assessment of the extent to which exam nerves are going to be a barrier to a fair test. The Examiner should, by their personal demeanour, put the candidate at ease and make sure that at no time does the test degenerate into a clash of personalities. Examiners must maintain an objective and professional outlook at all times.

The Examiner can unwittingly build up stress in a number of ways. He/she should be particularly careful to avoid, for instance:

■ Any remark which the candidate might interpret as being gratuitously disparaging.

■ Apparent secrecy about their intentions during the exam.

■ Prolonged periods of silence.

■ Quick-fire questions.

■ Irrelevant questions when the candidate is trying to concentrate on the task in hand.

Stress can be reduced by:

■ Setting a straightforward practical task and giving a genuine 'well done' at the end (assuming it was successful).

■ Taking an interest in the candidate and communicating in a non-confrontational way.

■ A sense of humour – but do not make the candidate the butt of the joke, and avoid sarcasm

■ Ensuring a suitable briefing is provided to candidates prior to the commencement of the exam.

Pass/Fail Decision

In deciding whether or not a candidate should pass or fail, a broad view of overall performance should be taken. No candidate is perfect and the Examiner must therefore balance the strengths and weaknesses when coming to a pass/fail decision. In making this decision the Examiner must heavily mark down any indication of unsafe practice, lack of knowledge or poor application of IPRCS.

Post-exam Debrief

The Examiner should debrief the candidate at the end of the exam. If the candidate has passed, the debrief can be quite short and provide praise where praise is due and feedback on areas for improvement if warranted.

If the candidate has not reached the standard in one or two small areas you may wish to reassess them on one or two of these areas whilst still afloat – in other words providing the candidate with a second chance for, say, one particular task prior to concluding the exam. This gives the candidate who you feel may disagree with your recommendation a chance to retry any parts of the test which they might feel gave an incorrect conclusion. It also makes the final debrief much easier. The candidate should be given a plan of how to improve in order to pass next time. Remember to praise the good points and be positive.

It is essential that the debrief is mirrored by what is written in the candidate's exam report. Remember also that in the event of a fail the candidate will receive a copy of the Examiner's report from the RYA.

Exam Reports

The exam report should provide a clear picture of what types of tasks were carried out in the exam as well as how the candidate fared in each category in which he/she was tested. Simply writing 'good' or 'satisfactory' is not acceptable. A couple of sentences outlining why you have deemed the candidate's performance as acceptable or otherwise are essential.

The Examiner should forward to the RYA Certification Department:

- Exam payment.
- Exam application form.
- Practical report.
- Passport photo.
- Verification of having sighted the candidate's SRC and First Aid (RYA First Aid Certificate or another acceptable First Aid certificate, as detailed on the RYA website) certificates.

If they require a Commercial Endorsement, please also forward the fee (see the RYA website), their ML5 medical report (original) and a copy of the Sea Survival certificate along with a copy of their PPR course completion certificate.

The RYA will issue the certificate of competence directly to the candidate.

Partial Re-examination

An Examiner may conduct a partial reassessment for a candidate who is a competent powerboat driver but has been deferred on a 'memory' part of the syllabus. A reassessment may not be given for boat handling, fundamental principles of navigation/IRPCS or for a lack of safety awareness. For anything more substantial than a single narrow area of deficiency the exam should be considered as a 'fail' and any subsequent examination should be a full exam conducted by a different Examiner.

Barriers to Examination

An Examiner should not examine a candidate who is a personal friend, someone whom they have taught or previously failed in an examination, or with whom they have any potential direct commercial relationship.

Examiners must examine only in boat types with which they have experience and which they would themselves be confident to skipper.

Part 3

The RYA Personal Watercraft Scheme

The RYA Personal Watercraft Scheme was developed when it became apparent that there was a requirement for a qualification or award to recognise competency in the use of personal watercrafts, or PWs. The popularity of these craft has been steadily growing over the past decades and they have now become a sport in their own right.

RYA-recognised centres can be for PWs only, but more commonly they are an integral part of an existing RYA powerboat school.

These schools are recognised to run the RYA Personal Watercraft Proficiency Course and, upon successful completion, candidates will receive the RYA Personal Watercraft Proficiency award.

Courses are taught by an RYA Personal Watercraft Instructor. Courses will be for no more than six candidates on three sit-down PWs with no more than two candidates per PW, or no more than three candidates with no more than one student per stand-up PW.

Courses will be predominantly practical. The emphasis of the course is on safe operation of a personal watercraft and, as such, should be 90 per cent afloat.

RYA Personal Watercraft Instructor Course

Courses are run at a number of centres around the world. The course will be run by an appointed RYA Personal Watercraft Trainer who has been trained and assessed to deliver the course to the required standard. Each course will be moderated on the last day by another, separate RYA Personal Watercraft Trainer, who will assist the course trainer in reaching a decision on the candidate's performance.

Candidates will need to hold the RYA Personal Watercraft Proficiency award and have at least two years' experience of riding personal watercrafts and hold a valid first aid certificate approved by the RYA. See the RYA website for details.

Syllabus

The RYA Personal Watercraft Instructor course is conducted over three days and will contain the following elements:

- The theory of teaching – principles of practical instruction.
- Delivering theory subjects.
- Preparation and effective use of visual aids.
- Lesson and programme planning.
- Teaching styles.
- Practical driving and driving skills.
- Reviewing and feedback skills.
- The standards required by the RYA.
- Assessing student ability.
- The structure of the RYA Personal Watercraft Scheme.
- The standard and content required for the 'orientation' exercise.
- Developing student skills along a progressive pathway.
- The requirements for running an effective RYA Personal Watercraft school, including conditions for recognition.

During the course the candidate will receive input from the trainer and also from the other candidates. They will be asked to show the following:

- Knowledge of the subject of personal watercrafts.
- Ability to deliver effective teaching sessions.
- Ability to safely and effectively organise multiple personal watercraft.
- Ability to teach effectively multiple students on a fleet of personal watercraft.
- Ability to demonstrate all elements of the RYA Personal Watercraft Proficiency award and the RYA Personal Watercraft Safety award.
- Ability to deliver at least one theory session ashore.
- Be able to demonstrate safety awareness for themselves and students throughout.

Candidates will be asked to teach three distinct groups on the course:

- Each other, i.e. the other candidates on the course.
- The course trainer/moderator.
- Real students or 'guinea pigs', who have been asked to attend to assist the course. These must not be paying students on a recognised course.

Course Moderation

In common with the RYA Powerboat Scheme, the course will be moderated by an external moderator (RYA Personal Watercraft Trainer) who has not been associated with the course. They will view the candidates and help decide on the overall course outcome. They will also review the course in general to ensure that it has adhered to the standards set by the RYA.

The moderator (and trainer) will be looking for the following:

- Effective teaching of practical aspects of the RYA Personal Watercraft syllabus, preferably with 'real' students.
- Effective delivery of a theory topic ashore.
- Delivery of an unprepared short presentation on any aspect of the syllabus.
- Demonstration of an understanding and ability to deliver basic orientation required for a simple pilotage plan.
- Demonstration of an awareness and application of safety aspects required for teaching multiple candidates on multiple personal watercraft.

Successful candidates will be issued with an RYA Personal Watercraft Instructor certificate, which will be valid if the following criteria are met:

- It is no more than five years since it was issued.
- The holder also holds a valid first aid certificate approved by the RYA. See RYA website for details.
- Certificates may be revalidated by obtaining and returning a completed revalidation form detailing teaching experience in an RYA-recognised centre. A minimum of 30 hours' teaching is required.
- If the certificate is more than two years out of date, the candidates will be expected to retake the course.

If no teaching experience is logged, the applicant may be requested to attend a reassessment at their own cost.

Syllabus

The syllabus format closely follows that of the RYA Powerboat Scheme in that there are three levels of teaching, i.e.:

Knowledge of the subject.

Understands the subject.

Can. The student can successfully carry out the task set by the Instructor.

(Please see the relevant section of this publication for greater details of the above.)

However, teaching the practical syllabus requires a different approach, principally due to the fact that the Instructor can only accompany one student on one PW at a time. This presents group control problems not present in powerboat teaching.

However, each manoeuvre should have the same structure for the candidate as found in the RYA Powerboat Scheme, i.e.:

Teaching Model
E – Explanation
D – Demonstration
I – Imitation
C – Correction
T – Training (or practice)
S – Summarise the session

Student Model
P – Planning
A – Approach
M – Manoeuvre
E – Escape

RYA Personal Watercraft Scheme – Practical

Teaching PWs brings different challenges that are not present when teaching powerboat skills. In powerboating, the Instructor will be in the boat with the students and is able to talk directly to them, offering instant feedback and, if necessary, taking charge of the powerboat if there are any problems.

With PWs, the Instructor may be responsible for up to six students on three PWs. Therefore, there are group control considerations that are not present in powerboating. Organising the group safely is as important as teaching the skills needed for riding a PW and the Instructor must pay close attention to this.

When introducing a new skill, the Instructor should consider where the students are positioned, if the area is safe and whether they can all see the skills being demonstrated without looking directly into the sun.

The Instructor should also consider the implications of having multiple students and PWs on-task at the same time.

Once students are riding 'solo', communicating with them becomes very difficult, so simple hand signals should be established and the understanding of them confirmed before students begin a task. Simple hand signals should include the following:

- Stop
- Come to me
- Slow down
- Speed up
- Turn to port
- Turn to starboard

Personal Watercraft Handling

Can:

- Demonstrate the correct use of the killcord at all times. **As with the RYA Powerboat Scheme,** correct use of the killcord is vital. Personal watercraft riders generally wear their killcord around the wrist. However, students should be encouraged to clip the wrist loop into their buoyancy aid/impact jacket. This removes any possibility of it accidentally slipping off.

- **Board a PW from shallow water and start the engine.** Students should align the PW so that it is facing away from the beach in waist-deep water. They should then board over the stern and move forwards into the steering position. They should then attach the killcord, start the PW and move away from the beach using idle speed only until they are clear and in deeper water.

- **Control a PW at slow speed using all gears and controls.** Students should be able to drive in a straight line, turn to port and starboard and come to a stop without using reverse (or the 'braking effect' fitted on some models), using the direction of drift only. They can ascertain the direction of drift by stopping the PW and seeing which way it is carried. They should also be familiar with and be able to use reverse and the 'braking effect', if the craft is equipped with them.

Teaching notes: As this may be the student's first time on a PW, the Instructor should give a short demo. The student will accompany the Instructor, sitting behind them. After the demo, where the PW has been returned to the beach, the Instructor will change places with the student, and the exercise repeated. It is recommended that the Instructor wears the killcord during the exercise.

The exercise will include: attaching killcord, stopping and restarting engine, moving slowly away from the beach, driving forward in a straight line, turns to port/starboard (with a visual check made before turning), stopping into the direction of drift (no reverse thrust or 'braking effect'), reversing (if fitted), use of 'braking effect' (if fitted). Return safely to the beach by turning parallel to it when waist deep and into the direction of drift to slow down. Switch off engine and step off the PW on the 'non-beach' side into deeper water if there are any waves.

The student can then repeat 'solo'. Be sure to check understanding of the task and establish simple hand signals to communicate with the student before the student leaves the beach.

If there are multiple students, they each wait for their turn for the task. Consequently, this section should only take a few minutes per student.

Stopping Distances

Aim: Demonstrate a practical understanding of stopping distances.

Planning: When teaching one PW, lay two buoys 15 metres apart. When teaching two or more PWs, lay a box course.

Exercise 1A (for PWs with RiDE or iBR):

Speed: Displacement.

Exercise 1B (for PWs with RiDE or iBR):

Speed: Planing. The student rides from buoy A to buoy B. Once adjacent to buoy B ask them to implement the electronic deceleration system. Observe the distance they have taken to stop.

Debrief: How much effect did the deceleration have? Pros and cons of electronic deceleration systems, e.g. bow drop, stopping distance, stability etc.

Exercise 2 (for PWs with RiDE or iBR):

Speed: Planing. The student rides from buoy A to buoy B, implementing the electronic deceleration system in order to achieve a stopped position adjacent to buoy B (this may take more than one attempt).

Exercise 3A (for all PWs):

Speed: Displacement.

Exercise 3B (for all PWs):

Speed: Planing. The student rides from buoy A to buoy B. Once adjacent to buoy B they press the stop button and allow the craft to drift to a rest. Observe the distance they have taken to stop.

Debrief: Discuss the difference in stopping distances between the two speeds and what additional effects are in play, e.g. tidal flow, wind effect, weight of PW, hull design.

Exercise 4 (for all PWs):

Speed: Planing. The student rides from buoy A to buoy B, reducing speed and pressing the stop button in order to obtain a stopped position adjacent to buoy B (this may take more than one attempt).

Teaching notes: Choose a safe, clear area to carry out the exercises. Ensure all riders have an opportunity to experience each exercise. If teaching multiple PWs, set up a box course in order to have two PWs carrying out exercise at the same time. Ensure PWs are both travelling in the same direction to ensure collision situations are not created (i.e. buoys A - B and buoys C - D). See example course layout diagram. If PW does not have RiDE or iBR technology, introduce these systems in theory.

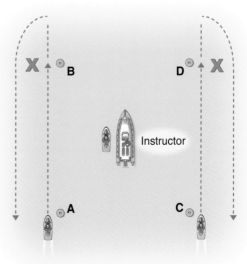

Come Alongside another Craft, Pontoon or Floating Dock

Aim: To bring the PW safely alongside a solid pontoon/dock without damage.

For brevity, only one method will be described. See RYA Powerboat Level 2 sections for other methods.

Note: The word 'dock' is being used throughout this exercise to represent another craft/pontoon/floating dock.

Planning

- Establish the direction of drift.
- Position the PW below the direction of drift and away from the dock.
- Prepare fenders and painter (if appropriate).
- Check for obstructions/other water users.
- Decide on what part of the dock is to be used.
- Plan escape route.

Approach

- From a position clear of the dock, begin a parallel approach into the direction of drift.
- Maintain slow speed using idle speed, but make progress against the direction of drift.
- Continue to check for obstructions and other water users.
- When the course allows an approach angle to the dock of 40–45 degrees, turn towards the pontoon.
- Maintain the approach angle by using transits. Note that the bow of the PW might not be pointing directly at the dock at this stage.

Manoeuvre

- Ensure that the approach speed is slow – idle speed may be too fast, so use neutral as required or stop/start the engine (if ski not fitted with reverse) to achieve correct speed.
- When within 1–2 PW lengths away from the dock, apply neutral or stop engine.
- Turn the steering full lock away from the pontoon.
- Into forwards gear briefly or start engine to push the stern of the PW towards the pontoon.
- Neutral or stop engine.
- Attach painter.

Escape

- While approaching, keep checking for obstructions/other water users.
- During approach, if an escape route is needed due to the approach course being at an angle, providing there is room, the PW can be turned safely away from the dock. Ensure that there is space for the stern to swing clear of the dock.

Leaving from Alongside a Craft, Pontoon or Floating Dock

Planning

- Ensure that it is clear all around.
- Check for obstructions/other water users.

Approach/Manoeuvre

- Release the painter.
- Reverse away carefully.
- If ski does not have reverse, push bow gently away from the pontoon.
- Ensure handlebars are in straight-ahead position.
- Once the bow is clear of the dock, start the engine and, at idle speed, drive away to a clear space.

Teaching notes: Although this exercise can be practised against a pontoon or floating dock, it is best taught using a safety craft. The tubes of the RIB provide a much better 'face' to come alongside than a pontoon, as PWs rarely carry fenders and they have few attachment points when they do. The Instructor should give a demonstration of the exercise with the student riding 'pillion'. The student and Instructor can then change places, and the student tries the manoeuvre. If successful, the student can try 'solo'. If teaching multiple students, the remaining students should be positioned so that they can safely and comfortably observe the demonstration. Once they are riding competently solo, the Instructor can set up a 'circuit', where all students are coming alongside one at a time.

Approach and Recover an MOB

Aim: To pick up a passenger who has fallen from the PW, or to pick up someone who is in the water.

Man overboard is taught as a 'drill' using a 'dummy' target to simulate a passenger falling off. The drill must never be taught with real people.

Planning

- In a clear area that will not interfere with other water users, prepare to throw over the MOB dummy.

Approach

- When safe to do so, throw the dummy target into the water.
- Driver will hold their course and reduce speed smoothly to 'dead slow' or idle speed.
- The PW travelling at idle speed should be brought around downwind of the target dummy to begin an upwind approach.

Manoeuvre

- Continue to approach the dummy. Speed should be 'dead slow'.
- Continue a dead-slow approach, using neutral as necessary or stop/start if PW has no gears.
- The PW should be positioned so that the dummy is presented to one side of the bow.
- Once close to the dummy, switch off the engine.
- Bring the dummy aboard the PW over the stern.

Escape

- The driver should be very aware of their approach speed towards the dummy.
- If they are unhappy with the speed or direction of their approach, the driver should abort their approach early.
- The PW can then be repositioned for another attempt.

Teaching notes: The Instructor will give a demonstration of the exercise, then change places with the student so that coaching can be given. If successful, the student can then try 'solo'.

Demonstrating Practical Application of the Rules of the Road

IRPCS

Students should be given a theory briefing on the collision regulations and how they relate to them riding PWs.

The minimum should include:

- Maintain a good, all-round lookout at all times.
- Drive at a safe speed at all times.
- Avoid all collision situations.
- Any action to avoid a collision should be taken early and should use an obvious and large alteration of course (and/or speed).
- Action for 'head on', 'overtaking' and 'crossing'. Give-way and stand-on situations should be explained. This knowledge should be thoroughly checked by the Instructor in a question & answer session using visual aids.

The Instructor will then run a practical session for the application of the Rules of the Road.

Rules of the Road

This exercise should be run around a box course, at a speed of 8–10 knots.

Once the students are riding round the course in a controlled, predictable manner, the Instructor rides onto the course in such a way that they create one of the potential collision situations discussed, i.e. head-on, overtaking or crossing (give way and stand-on).

If the students respond correctly to each situation, the Instructor should acknowledge this with a confirmation signal. If a student responds incorrectly, the Instructor should stop the exercise and provide appropriate feedback.

When teaching more than one PW, student PWs must maintain at least one buoy between them. They should never be on the same leg.

Group Control in Transit

The student should be instructed to follow the Instructor approximately five PW lengths behind and two PW lengths to one side. They should match the speed and direction of the Instructor, but should never cross their wake. Simple hand signals for speeding up/slowing down and turns to port/starboard should be agreed prior to the exercise. This allows the Instructor to make IRPCS decisions for the group while under way.

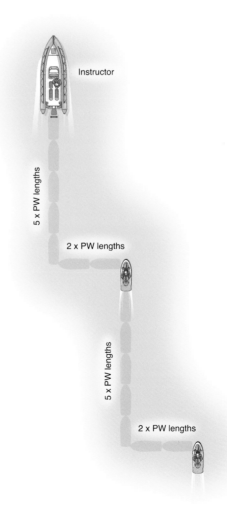

Instructor

5 x PW lengths

2 x PW lengths

5 x PW lengths

2 x PW lengths

Control and Corner a PW at Planing Speeds

Aim: To be able to ride the PW at higher speeds safely and under control. While at speed, the PW can be cornered in both directions in both long- and short-radius turns.

Plan: As the PW will be travelling faster and further, a large, open space, free from obstacles, should be used. Constant observation is required, particularly in the direction of a turn before it is executed.

Manoeuvre: The PW is more stable at speed, so once the student is used to travelling more quickly, they might find driving the craft easier. However, it will travel further at a higher speed, so vigilance and an all-round lookout is essential. Additionally, before making a turn, the driver should ensure all around is clear, particularly in the direction that they are turning.

Escape: Due to the manoeuvrability of PWs they are able to change direction quickly. If the driver is observant and anticipates the movements of other water users, a collision situation can easily be avoided. See teaching notes for more details.

Teaching notes:

- **First planing-speed ride:** The Instructor drives the PW with the student riding pillion. The Instructor will demonstrate getting onto and coming off the plane and the behaviour of the craft while it does so. They will also demonstrate planing-speed turns of various radii. The student and Instructor then change places and the student repeats. The Instructor should wear the killcord. While under way, the instructor makes all IRPCS decisions. The Instructor should dictate the course and speed from another craft (PW or RIB).

- **Box course:** The student can travel at planing speed and perform more challenging turns around a box course of four buoys. This simple course allows them to follow a predictable, predetermined course. The Instructor can position themselves in the middle of the box and control the student from there. Hand signals, direction of travel, which buoy to start from and when to start and stop will need to be agreed upon before beginning the exercise. If a student falls off their craft, they should first indicate to the Instructor that all is well and then reboard. If another student is on the course, this student should stop and wait at the next buoy they reach until the start or recall signal is given. It is recommended that NO planing takes place within the box.

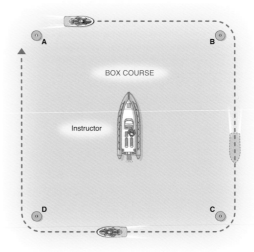

BOX COURSE

Instructor

Tasks

Fast straights, slow corners (acceleration/deceleration): The student (after being 'started' by the Instructor) may travel as quickly as they wish between buoys, but they must slow down and corner at displacement speed. They are then free to accelerate towards the next buoy, and so on. If two students are using the course, they must circulate in the same direction and must keep two buoys between themselves and the next student. If this becomes impossible, they must stop at the next buoy until they can. It is possible to have three students on the course. They must keep one buoy between them and the next student. There must never be two PWs on the same leg.

Fast straights, wide corners: After being 'started', the students may travel as quickly as they wish between the buoys and corner with a wide entry and exit. In reality, they will be almost travelling in a large circle around the course.

Fast straights, fast corners: After being 'started', the students may travel as quickly as they wish between the buoys, and corner as tightly and as quickly as they feel comfortable at the buoys. This may lead to a rider falling off; therefore, reinforce the 'stopping at the next mark' rule before the exercise begins.

Teaching notes: During these exercises, emphasis should be on rider's active body position, pillion actions, trim usage (where fitted), the speed management through corners (brake before, accelerate out).

Slalom Exercise

By moving one downwind corner buoy to the middle of the course, and replacing it with the Instructor PW or RIB, a simple slalom course is created. By positioning the RIB on the downwind corner, if it is drifting it travels away from the course, not towards it.

Using a student PW, the Instructor demonstrates to the students the course and the tighter turns that are required. They should emphasise that the slalom course finishes at the last buoy (buoy D in the diagram) and that they return towards the RIB/PW at displacement speed. The next student should not be released until the first student has returned and stopped. After practice, the students can have their runs timed by their Instructor.

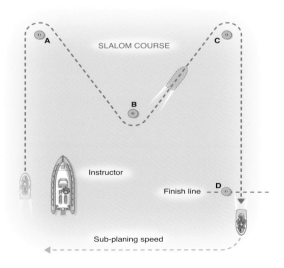

SLALOM COURSE

Instructor

Finish line

Sub-planing speed

Emergencies

Towing

Aim: To set up a tow between two PWs and be able to return the disabled PW to a safe point.

Can:

- Set up a tow using a bowline and a round turn & two half hitches.
- Tow another PW or craft.

Teaching notes: The towline, which should be of the floating type, should be attached to the aft towing eye of the towing PW using a round turn & two half hitches. The towline should then be attached to the bow eye on the disabled PW using a bowline. Some purpose-made towlines have clips already attached, making knots unnecessary. However, these clips will not pass through the towing eyes. In this case, a loop of rope or 'bight' is pushed through the eye and the clip goes onto this loop. Ideally, this should be achieved without entering the water, but take care not to get hands/limbs caught between the two PWs. Once attached, the line should be brought onto the towing PW to be paid out as the PW slowly moves away. Discuss the risk of hand injuries and the potential for the PW sucking up any loose line. Once the line is taut, speed can be gently increased to a brisk walking pace. Any faster could risk damaging the operating parts of the disabled PW.

Boarding a PW from Deep Water

If the rider falls off the PW, boarding should first simply be a matter of swimming back to the craft. Some PWs have a fold-down boarding bar to assist climbing back on. Most have a boarding/grab handle behind the seat to allow the rider to haul themselves back onto the PW. Care should be taken not to step on the jet nozzle. Once onboard, move forward on the craft, staying in balance. The killcord can then be reattached, the PW started and driven off.

Personal Watercraft Theory

Knowledge of:

- **Types of PW.** PWs fall into two main categories, 'Sit-on' and 'stand-up'. The names are self-explanatory. Sit-on PWs are by far the most common type, being easier to ride, able to take passengers and having a wide range available from the various manufacturers. Stand-up craft are more difficult to master and only take the rider. There is no room or provision for a passenger.
- **In-built technology.** Trim, no-wake mode, RiDE, iBR.

Understands:

- Layout of a PW:
    - **Controls.** These are mainly located on the handlebars. There will be a throttle (either finger- or thumb-operated), a start & stop button, a killcord-mounting position and, on most models, a reverse gear mechanism, a trim selector to change the ride angle of the PW when under way, and no-wake mode.
    - **Propulsion & steering system.** PWs are driven forward by a water jet. The more power that is applied, the more water is forced through a nozzle on the transom of the craft. This nozzle can be directed by the handlebars to give steerage. Some craft are fitted with a reverse thrust lever to allow them to operate astern propulsion.
    - **Fuel and oil.** Most PWs are now fitted with four-stroke engines, so do not need to have oil injected into the fuel to provide lubrication. The level can usually be checked with a dipstick. Fuel is added 'neat', i.e. without oil mixed, and the level can be checked with a fuel gauge most often found on the instrument panel.
    - **Stowage compartments.** PWs have several stowage compartments, usually in the bow, under the rear seat and a smaller one below the handlebars. Although these are protected from the water, they shouldn't be relied on to be watertight.
- Personal equipment:
    - Wetsuit/drysuit. The prevailing conditions will determine what clothing is most appropriate. As a minimum wetsuit shorts should be worn to protect from water-ingress injuries.
    - Personal buoyancy. In common with most water activities, personal buoyancy is required. Due to the speeds that PWs can reach, a standard buoyancy aid may not provide sufficient protection when the rider makes contact with the water if thrown off. Specialised impact jackets are recommended.
    - Foot and eye protection is recommended for reasons similar to those above.
    - Essential PW gear. This would include a towline, flare pack, waterproof torch, waterproof compass and chart, VHF marine radio, knife with serrated edge, fire extinguisher, small first aid kit, anchor and line, tool kit with spare spark plugs.
- Pre-launch check: A visual check of the craft to check for cracks in the hull or obvious damage, check of controls and their operation, start/stop engine (briefly), check killcord operation, oil and fuel level, all extra equipment is onboard and securely stowed, bungs in!
- Pre-departure checks: Slipway, launching area, parking for vehicle and trailer, anchoring or pontoon to berth craft while parking vehicle and trailer, informing someone ashore of intentions, ETD/ETA and what to do if no contact is made.
- Essential safety information, local hazards (check chart), safe speed and speed limits (chart and local bylaws).

Weather, Safety and Courtesy to Others

- Sources and significance of weather forecasts. Where to obtain a marine inshore forecast and why they would be of use.
- Avoiding pollution, disturbance, damage to wildlife and wildlife habitats. PWs can operate in shallow water, which could bring them into proximity of nesting birds and small mammals. Riders should be responsible in their driving and not enter such areas.

Understands:

- Interpreting a relevant forecast. This is likely to be an inshore forecast that contains wind strength (Beaufort scale) and direction, and visibility.
- Courtesy to other water users. PWs are fast and considered a nuisance by many water users. Give consideration to others when riding.
- Lee and weather shores. Lee (onshore winds) shores present problems for launching and landing. Care should be exercised when leaving or approaching them. Weather shores give a flat appearance, which is ideal for riding, but if the rider has mechanical difficulties the PW will be blown offshore.

Launching and Familiarisation

Knowledge of:

- Balance and trim. If the PW has the capability of changing the angle of trim then it should be used to give a slight 'bow-up' attitude when under way. This will promote earlier planing.

Understands:

- Launching from a trailer (see powerboat section).
- Anchoring. If the PW carries an anchor, the procedure is much the same as for powerboating (see relevant section).
- Stowing and securing to a trailer (see powerboat section).

Emergencies

Understands:

■ How to right a capsized PW. The rider should first go to the transom to check if there is a 'righting direction' arrow. The PW must be rotated upright in the direction indicated by the arrow only. Failure to do so could cause damage to the engine. Once the direction has been determined, the rider should go to the correct side of the PW. They should reach up to take hold of the intake grille that will be uppermost on the hull. By pulling on the grille and pressing down on the gunwale or rubbing strake, the craft should rotate upright. Remember to release the grille as the PW rotates.

■ Once upright, the rider can move to the transom and use the boarding step, if fitted. Care should be taken not to step on the jet nozzle while reboarding.

Rules of the Road

Knowledge of:

■ Sound signals. Riders should be aware of the following: one blast ('I am turning to starboard'), two blasts ('I am turning to port'), three blasts ('My engines are operating astern propulsion'), five blasts ('Make clear your intentions').

Understands:

■ Lookout. Riders should have all-round awareness at all times.

■ Safe speed. Although PWs are capable of reaching high speeds, PW riders have the same obligations regarding speed as any other water user.

■ Priorities between other classes of vessels. Riders should understand the hierarchy of vessels within the collision regulations and the position PWs have within them.

■ Head-on, overtaking and crossing rules. Riders should know the action to be taken by the stand-on and give-way vessels in these situations.

■ Local bylaws, speed limits and prohibited areas. These can be obtained from the local harbour authority. N.B. Some areas prevent the use of PWs entirely.

Essential Navigation

Knowledge of:

- Charts. The significance of the various colours, depths, soundings, contours, drying heights, and hazards.
- Buoyage. Laterals, cardinals, isolated dangers and special marks.
- Tides and tidal streams. The vertical and horizontal movement of water.

Understands:

- How to interpret tidal information. Be able to use a tide table to determine high and low water times and heights.

Can:

- Plan and follow a route using a compass.

Recovery and Aftercare

Knowledge of:

- Aftercare and basic maintenance. Be able to drain down the hull using bungs. Allow the engine compartment to dry. Treat all vital components with an anti-corrosion agent. Add lubricant to the appropriate parts. Check oil levels. Care for the battery and terminals.

Understands:

- How to recover a PW from the water (see powerboat section).
- How to prepare PW and associate gear for trailing (see powerboat section).

Part 4

The RYA Inland Waterways Scheme

Despite the UK being an island nation and its inhabitants never being far from the coast, the UK has access to over 3,000 miles of an interconnected waterways system. In the recent past this system fell into disuse and disrepair, but fortunately, due to the foresight of an active group of forward-thinking enthusiasts, large sections have now been saved for many future generations of boaters to enjoy.

Although the pace of the activity can be regarded as more leisurely than other branches of powerboating activity, it is no less rewarding and can offer much to the recreational boater.

RYA-recognised inland waterway centres are on the increase and those new to the activity, or those wishing to add to their skills, would benefit from the courses offered.

The teaching in these centres reflects the methods found in other branches of powerboating. Instructors may consider using EDICTS to teach their students. Students in turn might like to use PAME when executing skills and manoeuvres.

For the purpose of this publication, the exercises in the following sections will assume the use of a narrowboat or barge. The reasoning for this is that it would be considered the slowest, heaviest and least manoeuvrable craft of those found on inland waterways.

RYA Inland Waterways Instructor Course

Courses are run at a number of centres around the UK. Each course will be run by an appointed RYA Inland Waterways Trainer who has been trained and assessed to deliver the course to the required standard. Each course will be moderated on the last day by another, separate RYA Inland Waterways Trainer, who will assist the course trainer in reaching a decision on the candidate's performance.

The RYA Inland Waterways Instructor course is conducted over two days and will contain the following elements:

- The theory of teaching – principles of practical instruction.
- Delivering theory subjects.
- Preparation and effective use of visual aids.
- Lesson and programme planning.
- Teaching styles.
- Practical teaching and driving.
- Reviewing and feedback skills.

- The standards required by the RYA.
- Assessing student ability.
- Structure of the RYA Inland Waterways Scheme.
- Developing student skills along a progressive pathway.
- The requirements for running an effective RYA Inland Waterways school including conditions for recognition.

During the course the candidate will receive input from the trainer and also from the other candidates. They will be asked to show the following:

- Knowledge of the subject of inland waterways.
- Ability to deliver effective teaching sessions.
- Ability to demonstrate all elements of the RYA Inland Waterways Helmsman Course syllabus.
- Ability to deliver at least one theory session.
- Be able to demonstrate safety awareness for themselves and students throughout.

Candidates will be asked to teach three distinct groups on the course.

- Each other, i.e. the other candidates on the course.
- The course trainer/moderator.
- Real students or 'guinea pigs' who have been asked to attend to assist the course. These must not be paying students on a recognised course.

Course Moderation

The course will be moderated by an external moderator (RYA Inland Waterways Trainer) who has not been associated with the course. They will view the candidates and help decide on the overall course outcome. They will also review the course in general to ensure that it has adhered to the standards set by the RYA.

The moderator (and trainer) will be looking for the following:

- Effective teaching of practical aspects of the RYA Inland Waterways Helmsman Course syllabus, preferably with 'real' students.
- Effective delivery of a theory topic ashore.
- Delivery of an unprepared short presentation on any aspect of the syllabus.
- Demonstration of an understanding and ability to deliver basic navigation required for a pilotage plan.
- Demonstration of an awareness and application of the safety aspects required for inland waterways boating for all participants.

Successful candidates will be issued with an RYA Inland Waterways Instructor certificate, which will be valid for five years if supported by an approved valid first aid certificate.

The Instructor certificate will remain valid if the following criteria are met:

- It is no more than five years since it was issued.
- The holder also holds a valid first aid certificate approved by the RYA. See RYA website for details.
- Certificates may be revalidated by obtaining and returning a completed revalidation form detailing teaching experience in an RYA-recognised centre. A minimum of 30 hours' teaching is required.
- If the certificate is more than two years out of date, the candidates will be expected to retake the course.

If no teaching experience is logged, the applicant may be requested to attend a reassessment at their own cost.

General Considerations

Many boating aspects found on the inland waterways are found in the other boating activities. However, there are some specific differences that should be noted.

- Many of the waterways are tree-lined. This will mean that there may be overhanging branches that could be hazardous to crew members.
- Overhanging branches and shrubs may have discarded fishing tackle caught in them. This could mean unprotected hooks might snag crew while passing.
- Locks, bridges, tunnels and other structures are sited very close to the water's edge. This is quite normal, but crew must be aware of their presence and keep arms, legs and heads clear when passing them. As a guide, keep within the profile of the boat.
- If crew need to move around a narrowboat, for example when mooring, the safest route is through the boat, not along the outside.
- If crew need to move around the outside or the boat, use the grabrail – 'one hand for yourself – one hand for the boat'.
- Any boat poles or boathooks should be stowed well inboard, so they won't be grabbed by mistake when crew members are using the grab rails.
- Don't try to fend off using hands or legs. Vessels can be very heavy and a crew member is unlikely to be able to stop a boat making contact. Use a fender to cushion any contact.
- When moving from the boat to the bank, or vice versa, step. Don't jump.
- Narrowboats are slow to respond to control inputs. Make any steering or throttle input early to give the boat time to react.
- 'Propwalk': This is the sideways effect that a propeller has on a boat. It is most noticeable when going astern, but it is also present to a much lesser extent going ahead. When going

astern, as well as providing astern propulsion, 'propwalk' moves the stern sideways. It will only do this in one direction due to the rotation of the propeller in astern. Once this characteristic is known, it can be used to the helm's advantage to move the stern sideways when manoeuvring.

■ 'Bank effect' (interaction): This occurs when the boat is too close to a bank or another boat. Water being drawn into the propeller is accelerated between the two 'faces'. This can cause the boat to be 'drawn' toward the other face, overcoming the effect of the rudder. The solution is to slow down when in the proximity of the bank/another boat.

■ 'Reverse bank effect': This phenomenon occurs usually when coming alongside. As the stern nears the bank, the helm uses a burst of astern to slow the boat down. The water thrust forward by the propeller travels forward and 'bounces' off the bank, pushing the boat's stern out and away from the bank. The solution is to slow the boat down much earlier, almost to a standstill, then put the tiller over towards the bank and give a short burst of ahead to push the stern towards the bank.

■ Even though canal boats can be long and weigh many tons, like other boats, they are affected by the wind. Cross winds will blow the boat sideways across the canal and, if not corrected, into the opposite bank. Cross winds can be countered by 'crabbing' the boat slightly sideways, steering the bow gently into the wind. The effect of the wind can be very localised due to gaps in the trees or when the boat passes under a bridge, causing alternating gusts then shelter.

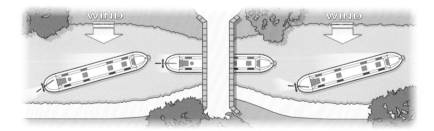

The wearing of lifejackets during training is strongly recommended. This is especially important when transferring to the bank and during lock and tunnel operations. Recognised Training Centres should have a clear policy on the use of lifejackets. They should be mindful of the mantra 'Useless unless worn'.

Coming Alongside – Using Crew

Aim: To bring the boat alongside the bank, either to moor or to drop crew off for passage of a lock or manual swing bridge, for example.

Success indicator: The boat stops as the bow makes contact with the bank. Stern is brought smoothly alongside with gentle or no contact. Crew is able to step ashore. Boat is secured effectively.

Planning: Choose a suitable space on the bank to come alongside. Check to see if there are bollards or mooring rings for the mooring line. If not, consider using a mooring stake (have a mallet ready). Brief crew of intentions and agree on any signals to be used. Check for any current. Crew goes forward to make ready the forward mooring line and fender. Prepare stern line on stern dolly. Plan an escape route.

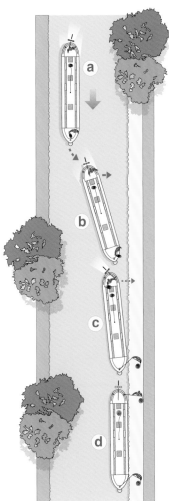

Approach: Slow the boat down by reducing power well before the intended mooring spot, but remain in gear to maintain steerage. Steer the bow in towards the intended stopping point on the bank (approximately 30 degrees). As the bow closes on the bank, pause in neutral then engage astern gear to slow the boat down.

Manoeuvre: The boat should stop as the bow touches the bank. Crew member steps ashore, takes turns around the bollard and then takes up the slack in the line. They then stand on the tail of the rope. On the confirmation signal from the crew member, the helm straightens the helm and first goes ahead, then steers the tiller towards the bank. This will begin to push the stern in towards the bank. As tension comes into the forward line, the stern will continue to swing towards the bank. As the stern arrives, the helm engages neutral and steps onto the bank with the stern line and makes it secure.

Escape: Use transits to judge approach speed. If too fast, increase astern power. Crew should not fend off. If the bow does not reach the bank, or is blown out, use small bursts of astern to draw back away from the bank. Use small bursts of ahead with the tiller in the appropriate direction to reposition the stern while doing so. Once straightened up, reposition the boat for the next attempt. Alternatively, when stepping onto the bank, the crew could take the centre line instead of the bow line. Once on the bank, they can assist the helm by gently pulling the boat towards the bank by the centre line. They should not secure it to a bollard if the boat is still moving, as the attachment point is high and it could cause the boat to tip unexpectedly.

Coming Alongside – Single-handed

Aim: To bring the boat alongside the bank without assistance from the crew.

Success indicator: The boat stops as the bow makes contact with the bank. Helm is able to step ashore. Stern is brought smoothly alongside with gentle or no contact. Boat is secured effectively.

Planning: Choose a suitable space on the bank to come alongside. Check to see if there are bollards. If not, consider using a mooring stake. Have a mallet ready. Check current. Prepare centre mooring line, leading it back along the cabin roof to the steering position. Prepare the stern line on the dolly. Plan an escape route.

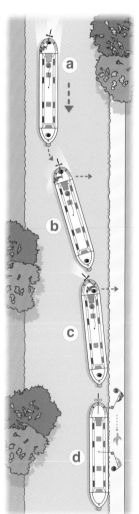

Approach: Slow the boat down by dropping power well before the intended mooring spot, but remain in gear to maintain steerage. Steer the bow in towards the intended stopping point on the bank (approximately 30 degrees). As the bow closes on the bank, engage astern to slow the boat down.

Manoeuvre: The boat should stop as the bow touches the bank. The helm straightens the helm and goes ahead, then steers the tiller towards the bank. This will begin to push the stern towards the bank. As the stern arrives, the helm engages neutral and steps onto the bank with the stern line and makes it secure. They then take the centre line and make this secure. They can secure the bow line if required, removing the centre line and coiling it ready for its next use.

Escape: Use transits to judge approach speed. If too fast, increase astern power. If the bow does not reach the bank, or is blown out by the wind, use small bursts of astern to draw back away from the bank. Use small bursts of ahead with the tiller in the appropriate direction to reposition the stern while doing so. Once straightened up, reposition the boat for the next attempt.

Leaving the Bank – Using Crew

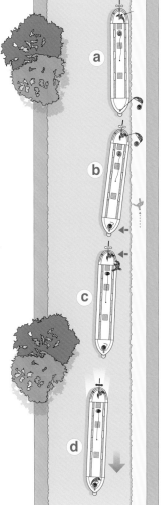

Aim: To leave the bank, having been secure alongside.

Success indicator: The boat is positioned in space in the canal/waterway, having made no contact on leaving, so that it can motor away safely.

Planning: Start the engine. Brief crew of intentions, check any signals to be used. Check the route is clear and there is no approaching traffic. Check wind direction and strength. Check depth of water. Plan escape.

Approach: Crew releases bow line from bollard/mooring stake/piling hook, but contact is maintained to prevent drifting.

Manoeuvre: Helm signals to crew. Crew puts line on board and gently pushes the bow out. Helm releases stern line and brings it on board. Meanwhile, the crew member walks back and steps aboard at the stern. With the tiller amidships, the helm engages ahead. They then push the tiller away from the bank. This will push the stern out from the bank. Once space has been made, they can centralise the tiller and gather way and steerage. Crew and helm tidy down the lines.

Escape: If there is any traffic, wait until it has passed.

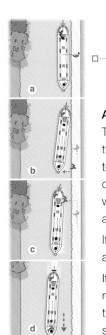

Alternatives: Instead of using a bow line, the crew can use the centre line. The crew can release the bow line, the helm can release the stern line and the crew can hold the boat alongside using the centre line only. When ready to leave, the crew moves forward, placing the centre line on the cabin roof near the bow, coiled ready for its next use. After communicating with the helm, they can then push the boat clear and board as described above.

If the water is shallow, the stern will need to be pushed, or preferably 'poled' away from the bank.

If the wind is blowing away from the bank, the bow and stern lines can be released simultaneously. Crew can step on board at the bow and tidy down the line. The wind will blow the boat away parallel from the bank. Once in a safe space, the helm can engage ahead and gather way.

Leaving the Bank – Single-handed

Aim: To leave the bank, having been secure alongside.

Success indicator: The boat is positioned in a space in the canal/waterway, having made no contact on leaving, so that it can motor away safely.

Planning: Start the engine. Check the route is clear and there is no approaching traffic. Check wind direction and strength. Check depth of water. Plan escape.

Approach: With the boat secured by the centre line, release and stow the stern line and bow line in sequence.

Manoeuvre: The helm walks forward and stows the coiled centre line on the cabin roof, near the bow, ready for its next use. They then push the bow out away from the bank, before walking back and boarding the boat at the stern. They then leave as described previously.

Escape: If there is any traffic, wait until it has passed.

Alternative: If the wind is blowing away from the bank, the bow line can be released first. The helm then goes back and boards the boat at the stern. They can then release and stow the stern line, before leaving as described previously.

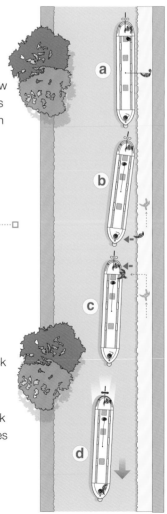

Leaving the Bank by 'Springing off' – Single-handed

Aim: To leave the bank using a stern spring line.

Success indicator: The bow of the boat is positioned in a space without the need for pushing from the crew, allowing the boat to motor away from the bank safely and making no contact while doing so.

Planning: Start the engine. Check the route is clear and there is no approaching traffic. Check wind direction and strength. Check depth of water. Ensure spring line attachment point on the bank (bollard, mooring ring or post) is secure enough. Plan escape.

Approach: Release bow line and stow securely on board. Walk to the stern. Cast off the stern line and walk forward 3–4 metres along the bank with it. Pass the line around the attachment point and take a turn around the stern dolly. The stern line is now set up as a 'slip' line, so that it can be released and retrieved easily from on board.

Manoeuvre: The helm steps on board. Holding the stern line (with a turn around the dolly), engage reverse and gently increase power. The bow will gently swing away from the bank. When a sufficient angle has been reached (15 degrees), the stern line is cast off and secured on board. The helm can then engage ahead and motor away.

Escape: If there is any traffic, wait until it has passed. Once the bow has swung out, it cannot be swung back in by reversing the procedure, so the helm must be sure they are ready and all is clear before starting the manoeuvre.

Turning using a Winding Hole

Aim: To turn the boat by 'fixing' the position of the bow against a purpose-built space in the bank.

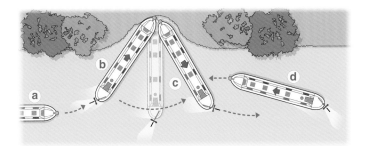

Success indicator: Turning the boat through 180 degrees in a confined space with contact at the bow only.

Planning: Choose a suitable winding hole well in advance of arriving opposite it. Not all winding holes will be long enough to allow certain boats to turn. A guide length will be found on a post on the bank opposite to the hole. Check which way the 'propwalk' is on the boat. Will it help or hinder?

Approach: As the hole is approached, reduce speed to dead slow. Steer the bow into the hole that is furthest from the opposite bank. Use reverse thrust to make very gentle contact with the bow on the bank.

Manoeuvre: With the tiller straight, gently apply power going ahead. Then move the tiller to the direction that the boat needs to turn. The stern will gently swing in that direction. Hold the tiller over until the turn is complete. Pause in neutral, then apply reverse gear to draw the boat back away from the bank. If the propwalk is helping, it will continue to swing the stern in the correct direction. If not, select neutral. Briefly apply a burst of power ahead and swing the tiller over to 'push' the stern in the required direction. Once straightened up, the helm can motor away in the new direction.

Escape: If, while turning, the turning action needs to be stopped, the helm simply has to straighten the tiller. This will 'hold' the boat at that point. When ready, the tiller can then be pushed over again to continue the turn.

Using Locks

Aim: To pass safely and effectively through locks both upstream and down.

Success indicator: The boat (and crew) transits the lock with minimal contact, leaving it ready for other users (and not losing the windlass).

Passing through locks is an integral part of using the inland waterways system. They allow vessels to travel up and down gradients using a series of 'steps' created by engineers. Although the passage will be slow, it is a charming characteristic of the waterways and is a pleasant and satisfying activity. However, it is not without dangers. Care must be taken when operating the machinery associated with the locks.

There are different types of lock depending on the canal and its location, but the general principle remains the same. A chamber has an entrance at each end that can be opened and closed with watertight gates. Water can be introduced or drained from the chamber when the gates have been closed. This filling or draining either raises or lowers the water in the chamber, and hence raises or lowers any vessel in the chamber.

General Considerations

- Crew will be moving on, off and around the boat. The wearing of lifejackets is strongly recommended.

- If the canal needs to be crossed, do so by a bridge or, if one is not available, the safest lock gate, which is the one away from the operating sluices.

- Once the sluices are operating, verbal communication becomes almost impossible. Agree on hand signals beforehand.

- Locks have cills. These will be marked. Ensure that the bow/stern is clear of them before changing the water level.

- Most sluice mechanisms will need to be operated with a 'windlass' handle. They don't float, so it should always be held onto securely.
- Lock gates are heavy. It's more efficient to push them than pull them.
- When opening a sluice the crew should stand away from the mechanism, so nothing can get caught in it.
- Once the opening/closing of the sluice is complete, remove the handle so that it can't fly off, causing injury.

When closing a sluice, the crew should hold the safety catch or pawl clear of the mechanism while winding the sluice closed. Never allow the sluice to drop as it could damage the mechanism.

Planning: Before the lock, come alongside. Agree on any hand signals and then drop a crew member off on the bank. They can then go ahead and prepare the lock(s). Maintain a 'safety gap' between them and the boat.

- If going 'uphill', the bottom lock should be empty and the rest in the flight full. If going 'downhill', the top one should be full and the rest empty.

Approach: The gates should be opened and the boat gently driven in. Once inside the lock, it can be held alongside with a line, usually the centre line. This should pass through a ring or around a post and held, but never tied off. A gentle 'nudge' ahead or astern can also be used. Ensure the bow/stern is clear of the cill. Once the helm is ready, they can signal to the crew to operate the sluices.

Manoeuvre: The crew operates the sluices appropriate to the position of the boat, relative to the expected water flow. This means that the moving water helps to hold the boat against the lock wall. The sluice should only be opened part way, to reduce the force of the moving water. As the water level changes, the effect of the flow is reduced and the sluices can be opened further.

Escape: If any problems occur during the lock operation, it is most important that the water movement is stopped by closing the sluices. Once this has been done, then the problem can be addressed.

Man Overboard

Performing a man-overboard manoeuvre similar to that found elsewhere in the RYA Powerboat Scheme with a canal boat would be impractical. In most situations, it would be impossible to turn the boat around and make an approach to pick up the person, as would normally be the case. Therefore it would be prudent to have measures in place in case it occurs, but, better than that, apply preventative measures to prevent the worst happening.

- When moving along or around the boat, try to do so inside the boat, rather than along the outside.
- If moving along the outside is unavoidable, use the 'one hand for the boat – one hand for yourself' rule.
- Wear non-slip footwear.
- If at all in doubt, wear a personal flotation device.
- When moving from the boat to the bank and vice versa, step. Don't jump.
- Consider having guard ropes in place to secure gaps at the bow and stern.
- Plan all manoeuvres well ahead, so rushing is avoided.
- Establish clear communication and signals between helm and crew.
- Have life rings or a buoyant 'horseshoe' easily accessible along the cabin roof.
- Have a buoyant throwline or lines readily available on the cabin roof.
- Practise throwing the line to a target, before you need to for real!

If the worst happens and someone does fall in, the following procedures should be used:

Success indicator: Not losing a person overboard! If, however, that does occur, they are brought to the bank or boat and recovered quickly and efficiently.

Narrow Canals and Waterways

- Select neutral and turn engine off.
- If available (and it should be), throw the person a life ring or throwline.
- Encourage the person to try standing up. Canals are very often shallow enough to allow this. They can then walk to the bank.
- Start the engine and put the boat alongside the bank and make fast. Use the adage, 'reach, throw, wade, swim' to recover the person. Swim is the LAST resort.

Locks

- Due to the restricted space in a lock, manoeuvring the boat is not an option.
- Shut down the sluices to stop the flow of water into or out of the lock.
- Turn the engine off.
- Secure the boat so that it cannot swing into the person and crush them.
- Reach with a pole or throw a lifering/throwline.
- Draw the person across to the ladder to allow them to climb out (every lock should have one).
- If they cannot climb out, **slowly** filling the lock to bring them up to the level of the bank may have to be considered as an option.
- Lock-keepers have all received training in rescue techniques, so if in attendance they will be able to offer assistance.

Wider Rivers and Estuaries

Narrowboats and barges move slowly in comparison to other vessels, so if someone falls overboard they are unlikely to be far from the vessel. Therefore, as in other situations, it will most likely be easier and quicker to be able to reach the person with a pole, lifebuoy or throwline. Having these devices readily available and to hand is strongly advised.

If there is room and the person is out of reach:

- Turn the boat round.
- Send crew forward through the boat to be ready to make contact with MOB.
- Face the boat into the current.
- Make slow approach, as for other MOB situations.
- Aim to make contact with the person to one side of the bow.
- Ensure that when contact is made the boat is stopped in the water.
- Engage neutral and consider stopping the engine.
- Go forward to assist crew.
- Bring MOB back on board.

Anchoring

There are only a few situations on canals and the inland waterway system where anchoring is necessary. The easier and more convenient thing to do would be to moor-up alongside the bank. In fact, anchoring in the middle of the canal or waterway would cause great inconvenience to other water users and therefore is not encouraged.

However, as in other boating situations, anchoring may have to be used in an emergency, e.g. engine failure, where fixing the position of the boat becomes a priority to prevent it drifting into any danger.

- Prepare the anchor on the 'up-current' end of the boat.
- Lower the anchor overboard, counting out how much line or 'scope' is paid out as the anchor touches bottom.
- Pay out the line to six times the depth of the water.
- Make the line secure on the dolly.
- Check that the anchor is holding using transits.
- Attend to the emergency.
- Move the boat to the bank as soon as is practical. The boat will be causing an obstruction to other water users.

Theory

Personal Safety

Understands:
- The risks involved with ending up in the water, including cold shock.
- Avoidance of personal injury, including crush injuries when fending off.
- Special risks to children.

Can:
- Correctly fit a buoyancy aid or lifejacket.

Engines

Understands:
- Checks to be undertaken periodically.

Can:
- Undertake checks to be carried out before and while running.

Deckwork

Knowledge of:
- Common boating terms.

Can:
- Handle warps and fenders (if used).
- Throw a heaving line or coiled rope.
- Tie the following:
  - Clove hitch.
  - Round turn & two half hitches.
  - Bowline.
- Secure to:
  - Bollards.
  - Rings.
  - Cleats.
  - Mooring stakes.

Helming and Boat Handling

Knowledge of:

- Berthing and unberthing between piles.

Understands:

- Loading and weight distribution.
- Inter-action and canal effect.
- Anchoring.
- Pivot points.

Can:

- Carefully steer a vessel.
- Turn a vessel around.
- Berth alongside.
- Recover a man overboard dummy.

Locks

Understands:

- Maintenance of levels.

Can:

- Operate a lock.
- Tend lines in a lock.

Bridges and Tunnels

Understands:

- Bridge operations.
- Use of tunnels.

Collision Avoidance

Knowledge of:

- The Rules of the Road.

Understands:

- Bylaws and local traffic regulations.
- National regulations.
- Publications to be carried.

Boat Safety

Knowledge of:

- Use of fire extinguishers.
- Watertight integrity.

Understands:

- Fire hazards, particularly gas and petrol.
- Refloating after grounding.

Care of the Environment

Understands:

- Avoiding damage to banks, boats, flora and fauna.
- Pollution avoidance.
- Consideration for water users.

Part 5

RYA Powerboat Pre-Instructor Skills Assessment Record

Candidate Name	
Centre	
Date of Course	
Course Trainer's Name *(print clearly)*	
Course Trainer's Signature	

RYA Power Schemes Instructor Log

Date	Boat type & Engine	Hours' Instructing	Course Level	Weather	Training Centre

Date	Boat type & Engine	Hours' Instructing	Course Level	Weather	Training Centre

Date	Boat type & Engine	Hours' Instructing	Course Level	Weather	Training Centre

Appendix 1 – Safeguarding and Child Protection

Introduction

RYA Recognised Training Centres that teach children and young people aged under 18 are required to have a formal safeguarding and child protection policy which is checked as part of their annual inspection.

Your organisation is therefore strongly advised to take the following steps:

- Adopt a policy statement that defines the organisation's commitment to providing a safe environment for children.
- Produce a simple code of practice and procedures governing how the organisation runs.

The RYA publishes guidelines to help clubs, training centres, and Instructors to enable children and vulnerable adults to enjoy the sports of sailing, windsurfing, and powerboating in all their forms in a safe environment. The policy, guidelines, and other best practice guidance can be downloaded from the RYA's website www.rya.org.uk/go/safeguarding and adapted to meet the requirements of your organisation.

The RYA Policy Statement on Safeguarding is as follows:

For England, Wales, and Northern Ireland this policy refers to anyone under the age of 18 as defined by the Children Act 1989 and The Children (Northern Ireland) Order 1995 and anyone aged 18 or over who is an 'Adult at Risk', who is in need of care or support, and who, because of those needs, is unable to always safeguard themselves as defined by the Care Act 2014 . For Scotland, the act defines adults at risk as those aged 16 years and over who:

- Are unable to safeguard their own wellbeing, property, rights, or other interests.
- And are at risk of harm.
- And because they are affected by disability, mental disorder, illness, or physical or mental infirmity, are more vulnerable to being harmed than adults who are not so affected.

The RYA is committed to safeguarding all children, young people, and adults at risk taking part in its activities from abuse and harm and ensuring their wellbeing. The RYA recognises that the safety, welfare, and needs of children, young people, and adults at risk are paramount and that any person, irrespective of their age, disability, race, religion or belief, marital status, sex, gender identity, sexual orientation, or social status, has a right to protection from discrimination and abuse.

The RYA takes all reasonable steps to ensure that, through safe recruitment, appropriate operating procedures, and training, it offers a safe and fun environment to children, young people, and adults at risk taking part in RYA events and activities. The RYA recognises that it has a legal responsibility to safeguard children, young people, and adults at risk, including due regard to the need to prevent people from being drawn into extremism and terrorism (the Prevent Duty).

The RYA is committed to minimising risk and supporting venues, programmes, events, and individuals to deliver a safe, positive, and fun boating experience for everyone by creating a welcoming environment, both on and off the water, where everyone can have fun and develop their skills and confidence. The RYA will treat everyone with respect, celebrate their achievements, listen to their views and experiences, and provide opportunities for all to fulfil their potential and be their authentic selves.

Through the RYA training scheme, the RYA is responsible for recognising Training Centres to deliver the RYA Training Scheme, and through its affiliation scheme, for providing advice and guidance for affiliated clubs and class associations. The RYA uses its position to require Recognised Training Centres to adopt and implement appropriate safeguarding policies and procedures and through its affiliation scheme encourages and supports affiliated organisations to do so by providing them with information, guidance and support.

The RYA:

- Recognises that safeguarding of vulnerable groups is the responsibility of everyone, not just those working directly with them.

- Carries out safe recruitment practices when recruiting all RYA employees, contractors and volunteers in roles involving close contact with vulnerable groups.

- Provides comprehensive training and personal development opportunities for all staff and volunteers, irrespective of their position, to ensure that any concerns are reported in a timely manner and to the right person.

- Responds swiftly and appropriately to all complaints and concerns about poor practice or suspected abuse, referring to external agencies as necessary.

- Provides signposting advice and guidance to anyone who needs it.

- Offers basic safeguarding advice and guidance to anyone within the boating community irrespective of if their club or centre is affiliated or recognised and gives full access to the safeguarding pages on the website to anyone wishing to access it.

- Regularly reviews safeguarding procedures and practices in the light of experience or to take account of legislative, social, or technological changes.

- Communicates changes and shares good practice with other NGBs, Recognised Training Centres, affiliates, and class associations.

- Encourages all RYA affiliates and class associations to adopt both a safeguarding children and young people policy and a safeguarding adults at risk policy.

- Ensures that all Recognised Training Centres have an in date Safeguarding and Protecting Children and Young People policy which is in line with the RYA's.

- Strives to achieve the highest level of safeguarding practices in line with the Child Protection in Sport Unit and Ann Craft Trust safeguarding standards and will undertake annual reviews of our policies and procedures to ensure full compliance with the standards.

- Provides mental health and wellbeing support to all staff through the colleagues' wellbeing programme.

- Will cooperate where necessary with multi-agency investigations and enquiries relating to serious case reviews involving children, young people, and adults at risk , if there is an association with the sport.

This policy will be reviewed by the RYA Safeguarding Steering Group annually and by the RYA Board at least every three years, or sooner if there are relevant legislative changes.

If you have a concern, allegation, or complaint please visit www.rya.org.uk/about-us/contact-us/comments-and-complaints.

Safe Recruitment and Criminal Records Disclosure Checks

The RYA is committed to ensuring that only those with the right motivations and suitability are recruited into positions involving regular contact with children, young people and adults at risk within its work and volunteer force. The RYA understands its legal responsibility within the Safeguarding Vulnerable Groups Act 2006, to ensure that all its recruitment practices are safe, fair, and equal and allows it to identify, deter, and reject applicants who may be at risk of abusing vulnerable groups.

The RYA will:

Ensure the best possible staff and volunteers are recruited based on their merits, abilities, and suitability for the position advertised.

Ensure that all applicants are considered equally and consistently, and that no applicant is treated unfairly based on any protected characteristics in compliance with the Equality Act 2010.

Comply with all relevant legislation, recommendations, and guidance including the statutory guidance published by the DfE (Keeping Children Safe in Education, the PREVENT Duty guidance) and any codes of practice published by any of the disclosure service providers used by the RYA (DBS, AccessNI, and PVG).

Meet its commitment to safeguarding and promoting the welfare of children, young people, and adults at risk by carrying out all necessary pre-employment checks.

The RYA uses the following safe recruitment practices when recruiting staff:

- Advertisements will make clear the commitment to safeguarding children, young people and adults at risk.

- Application forms are used which contain questions surrounding employment and academic history and a person's suitability for the role which includes the requirement to explain any gaps or discrepancies in the employment or academic history.

- The application form has a declaration regarding convictions and working with vulnerable groups and will make it clear if the post is exempt from the provisions of the Rehabilitation of Offenders Act 1974.

- CVs only will not be accepted.
- All job descriptions are clear and concise and accurately set out the duties and responsibilities of the job/volunteer role.
- Three references are requested alongside a job offer and a minimum of two must be received and reviewed before the candidate commences their role.
- All offers of employment will be subject to the receipt of a minimum of two references which are considered satisfactory by the RYA.
- Interviews are face-to-face where possible with a minimum of two interviewers and will cover the person's suitability for the role.
- All senior managers, recruiting staff/volunteers and HR personnel will undertake safe recruitment training which is refreshed every three years.
- All applicants invited to attend an interview will supply proof of their ID in the form of original documents and confirm their right to work within the UK.
- Where any position amounts to "regulated activity" an appropriate disclosure check will be carried out which will include the Children's Barred List where appropriate and an original certificate will be seen by the recruiting manager or HR personnel prior to the applicant commencing the role.
- Successful applicants in England and Wales will be encouraged to register with the DBS Update Service.
- Additional checks will be carried out if the applicant has lived or worked outside of the UK (certificate of good conduct, certificate of Sponsorship).

Criminal Records Disclosures

Organisations affiliated to or recognised by the RYA can access the DBS (previously CRB), Access NI, or PVG processes through the RYA which is a registered Umbrella/Intermediary Body. The procedure varies according to the home country and legal jurisdiction in which your organisation is located. Full information is available from the RYA website www.rya.org.uk/go/safeguarding or by contacting the RYA's Safeguarding and Equality Manager at disclosure@rya.org.uk.

Safeguarding Culture and Best Practice

The RYA considers the safeguarding of vulnerable groups to be the highest of priorities and, as such, is dedicated to ensuring that the RYA culture has safeguarding at its heart by incorporating policies, procedures, training, the use of best practice, and acting in accordance with RYA values to ensure that the most vulnerable groups are always protected. The RYA is committed to embedding safeguarding in everything it does, not only protecting vulnerable groups but also protecting its staff, volunteers, and contractors from putting themselves in potentially risky situations. There are many areas where best practice can be adhered to.

Additional best practice can be found in the RYA Safeguarding and Protecting Children Policy and Guidelines for Clubs, Centres and Class Associations and the RYA Safeguarding Adults Policy and Guidelines for Clubs, Centres and Class Associations. Both of these policies can be accessed on the RYA website: www.rya.org.uk/about-us/policies/safeguarding.

Responsibilities of Staff and Volunteers

Staff or volunteers should be given clear roles and responsibilities. They should be aware of your organisation's safeguarding policy and procedures and be given guidelines on:

- Following good practice.
- Recognising signs of abuse.
- Reporting any concerns to the appropriate person.

Identifying and Recognising Abuse

Please refer to Appendix A: What is Child Abuse? within the RYA Safeguarding and Protecting Children Policy and Guidelines for Clubs, Centres and Class Associations. Please also refer to Appendix A: What is Abuse? within the RYA Safeguarding Adults Policy and Guidelines for Clubs, Centres and Class Associations. Both of these policies can be accessed on the RYA website: www.rya.org.uk/about-us/policies/safeguarding.

Dealing with a Safeguarding Disclosure and Information Sharing

Being the recipient of a safeguarding disclosure can be incredibly difficult, especially if the recipient is not a Safeguarding Lead. However, choosing not to respond to a disclosure can never happen, regardless of how uncomfortable the recipient is. The referral flowcharts found within the two policies: RYA Safeguarding and Protecting Children Policy and Guidelines for Clubs, Centres and Class Associations and the RYA Safeguarding Adults Policy and Guidelines for Clubs, Centres and Class Associations should be used as a guide to the physical steps that can be taken if a referral or disclosure is received. Both of these policies can be accessed on the RYA website: www.rya.org.uk/about-us/policies/safeguarding. Below is a list of dos and don'ts to support someone in the moment that they receive a disclosure.

Dos

- Keep calm and remain receptive and approachable.
- Assess the situation, has a crime been committed? Do you need to contact the emergency services?
- Listen carefully and patiently without interrupting if possible and let the victim recount the details in their own time.
- Use the victim's own words if you need to seek clarification.

- If you need more information, use TED: Tell me... Explain to me... Describe to me...
- Acknowledge how difficult it must have been to disclose.
- Reassure them that they have done the right thing in telling you and they are not to blame.
- Let them know that you will do everything you can to help them.
- Advise the victim what will happen next.
- Make a written record as soon as you can.
- Report the disclosure to the Safeguarding team.
- Adults: Always involve the adult in any decision making regarding the referral and gain consent from the victim to share the information. If you feel that the adult does not have sufficient capacity to make a decision about sharing information, you should consider if breaking confidentiality is in the best interests of the victim. Please see the Mental Capacity and Consent section of the RYA Safeguarding Adults Policy and Guidelines for Clubs, Centres and Class Associations. This can be accessed on the RYA website: www.rya.org.uk/about-us/policies/safeguarding.
- Children and young people: Gain consent from the parent/carer to share the information. Only speak with the parents/caregivers of the victim if this does not pose a risk to the child.
- Use a person-centred approach.

Don'ts

- Don't make promises to keep secrets.
- Don't ask leading questions or put words in the mouth of the victim.
- Don't repeatedly ask the victim to repeat their disclosure.
- Don't discuss the referral with anyone who does not need to know.
- Don't be judgmental.
- Never ignore what you have been told or pass it on.
- Don't confront or contact the Subject of Concern.
- Don't remove or contaminate any evidence that may be present.
- Never dismiss your concerns – even a gut feeling is worth reporting.

Confidentiality

The sharing of personal information within an organisation is not prevented by law. While appropriate confidentiality should be maintained, it is important to make sure the right people within the organisation are informed if the circumstances require this. If you are the recipient of a safeguarding disclosure, contact the Safeguarding Manager who will advise on the next steps, which may or may not include sharing that information with external agencies, however the following considerations should be taken into account.

Confidentiality: Children and Young People

Information sharing is essential for effective safeguarding and promoting the welfare of children and young people. It is a key factor identified in many Serious Case Reviews (SCRs), where poor information sharing has resulted in missed opportunities to take action that keeps children and young people safe.

There are seven golden rules to confidentiality and Information Sharing:

1. Remember that the General Data Protection Regulation (GDPR), Data Protection Act 2018, and Human Rights law are not barriers to justified information sharing but provide a framework to ensure that personal information about living individuals is shared appropriately.

2. Be open and honest with the individual (and/or their family where appropriate) from the outset about why, what, how, and with whom information will, or could, be shared, and seek their agreement, unless it is unsafe or inappropriate to do so.

3. Seek advice from other practitioners, or the RYA Data Protection Officer, if you are in any doubt about sharing the information concerned, without disclosing the identity of the individual where possible.

4. Where possible, share information with consent, and where possible, respect the wishes of those who do not consent to having their information shared. Under the GDPR and Data Protection Act 2018 you may share information without consent if, in your judgement, there is a lawful basis to do so, such as where safety may be at risk. You will need to base your judgement on the facts of the case. When you are sharing or requesting personal information from someone, be clear on the basis upon which you are doing so. Where you do not have consent, be mindful that an individual might not expect information to be shared.

5. Consider safety and well-being: base your information sharing decisions on considerations of the safety and well-being of the individual and others who may be affected by their actions.

6. Necessary, proportionate, relevant, adequate, accurate, timely and secure. Ensure that the information you share is necessary for the purpose for which you are sharing it, is shared only with those individuals who need to have it, is accurate and up to date, is shared in a timely fashion, and is shared securely.

7. Keep a record of your decision and the reasons for it – whether it is to share information or not. If you decide to share, then record what you have shared, with whom, and for what purpose.

Confidentiality: Adults at Risk

Individuals may not give their consent to the sharing of safeguarding information for several reasons. For example, they may be frightened of reprisals, they may fear losing control, they may not trust social services or other partners, or they may fear that their relationship with the abuser will be damaged. Reassurance and appropriate support along with gentle persuasion may help to change their view on whether it is best to share information.

If a person refuses intervention to support them with a safeguarding concern, or requests that information about them is not shared with other safeguarding partners, their wishes should be respected. However, there are several circumstances where the practitioner can reasonably override such a decision, including:

■ The person lacks the mental capacity to make that decision – this must be properly explored and recorded in line with the Mental Capacity Act.

■ Other people are, or may be, at risk, including children.

■ Sharing the information could prevent a crime.

■ The alleged abuser has care and support needs and may also be at risk.

■ A serious crime has been committed.

■ Staff are implicated.

■ The person has the mental capacity to make that decision, but they may be under duress or being coerced.

■ In cases of domestic abuse, if the risk is unreasonably high and meets the criteria for a multi-agency risk assessment conference referral.

■ A court order or other legal authority has requested the information.

If none of the above apply and the decision is not to share safeguarding information with other safeguarding partners, or not to intervene to safeguard the person:

■ Support the person to weigh up the risks and benefits of different options.

■ Ensure they are aware of the level of risk and possible outcomes.

■ Offer to arrange for them to have an advocate or peer supporter.

■ Offer support for them to build confidence and self-esteem if necessary.

■ Agree on and record the level of risk the person is taking.

■ Record the reasons for not intervening or sharing information.

■ Regularly review the situation.

■ Try to build trust and use gentle persuasion to enable the person to better protect themselves.

If it is necessary to share information outside the organisation:

■ Explore the reasons for the person's objections – what are they worried about?

■ Explain the concern and why you think it is important to share the information.

■ Tell the person who you would like to share the information with and why.

■ Explain the benefits, to them or others, of sharing information – could they access better help and support?

- Discuss the consequences of not sharing the information – could someone come to harm?
- Reassure them that the information will not be shared with anyone who does not need to know.
- Reassure them that they are not alone, and that support is available to them.

If the person cannot be persuaded to give their consent, then, unless it is considered dangerous to do so, it should be explained to them that the information may be shared without consent in some situations (as set out above). The reasons should be given and recorded. The safeguarding principle of proportionality should underpin decisions about sharing information without consent, and decisions should be on a case-by-case basis.

If it is not clear that information should be shared outside the organisation, a conversation can be had with the Data Protection Officer or the safeguarding partners in the police or local authority without disclosing the identity of the person in the first instance. They can then advise on whether full disclosure is necessary without the consent of the person concerned.

It is very important that the risk of sharing information is also considered. In some cases, such as domestic violence or hate crime, it is possible that sharing information could increase the risk to the individual. Safeguarding partners need to work jointly to provide advice, support, and protection to the individual to minimise the possibility of worsening the relationship or triggering retribution from the abuser.

SafeLives (www.safelives.org.uk – previously CAADA) provide resources for identifying the risk victims face including a Dash risk checklist, which is a risk assessment tool for practitioners who work with adult victims of domestic abuse. It offers a consistent approach to identifying those who are at high risk of harm and whose cases should be referred to a MARAC (multi-agency risk assessment conference) meeting in order to manage their risk. If there are concerns about a risk to a child or children, then a referral to ensure that a full assessment of their safety and welfare needs to be made.

What to Do if You Are Concerned About a Child or About the Behaviour of a Member of Staff

A complaint, concern, or allegation may come from a number of sources: a child, their parents, or someone within your organisation. It may involve the behaviour of a volunteer or employee, or something that has happened to the child outside the sport, perhaps at home or at school.

An allegation may range from mild verbal bullying to physical or sexual abuse. If you are concerned that a child may be being abused, it is NOT your responsibility to investigate further BUT it is your responsibility to act on your concerns and report them to the appropriate statutory authorities.

If you're not sure what to do and need advice, you can call the RYA Safeguarding Manager on 023 8060 4104 or the NSPCC's free 24-hour helpline on 0808 800 5000.

Appendix 2 – Appeals Procedure

A candidate has grounds for appeal if he or she believes:

■ That they have not been given a reasonable opportunity to demonstrate their competence

or

■ That the person carrying out the assessment has placed them under undue or unfair pressure

or

■ That the trainer/moderator has reached the wrong conclusion on the basis of the outcome of the candidate's performance in the assessment.

The Procedure

The candidate should first raise the concern with the trainer/moderator to see if the matter can be amicably resolved. If it is inappropriate to consult the trainer/moderator, or if there is no amicable solution, the candidate should appeal in writing to the RYA Chief Instructor, Power, within 20 working days of the assessment. The letter of appeal should contain the following:

■ Full details of the assessment – when, where, involving whom etc.

■ The nature of the appeal.

■ Any supporting documentation relating to the assessment – outcome, action plans, reports etc.

On receipt of an appeal, an investigative process will commence. Following investigation, the candidate will be informed of the outcome, which will be one of the following:

■ The original decision confirmed.

■ The assessment carried out again by the same or a different trainer/moderator.

■ The original decision overturned and the assessment judged to be adequate.

If the candidate is still unhappy about the decision, they may appeal against the outcome to the RYA Training Committee.

Appendix 3 – Resources and References

You may find the following publications useful for further reading. All products can be purchased through the RYA webshop (www.rya.org.uk/shop).

Title	Author(s)	RYA Order Code
RYA Day Skipper Shorebased Notes	RYA	DSN
RYA Day Skipper Practical Course Notes	RYA	DSPCN
RYA Introduction to Motorboat Handling	Jon Mendez	DVD28
RYA Advanced Motorboat Handling	Jon Mendez	DVD29
RYA International Regulations for Preventing Collisions at Sea	Melanie Bartlett	G2
RYA Navigation Handbook	Melanie Bartlett	G6
RYA Navigation Exercises	Chris Slade	G7
RYA Powerboat Handbook	Paul Glatzel	G13
RYA Safety Boat Handbook	Laurence West Grahame Foreshaw	G16
RYA European Waterways Regulations	Tam Murrell	G17
RYA Powerboat Scheme Syllabus & Logbook	RYA	G20
RYA Diesel Engine Handbook	Andrew Simpson	G25
RYA VHF Handbook	Melanie Bartlett	G31

Title	Author(s)	RYA Order Code
RYA Introduction to Radar	Melanie Bartlett	G34
RYA Personal Watercraft Handbook	RYA	G35
RYA Tom Cunliffe's Manual of Seamanship	Tom Cunliffe	E-G36
RYA Start Powerboating	Jon Mendez	G48
RYA Knots, Splices & Ropework Handbook	Gordon Perry Steve Judkins	G63
RYA Yachtmaster Handbook	James Stevens	G70
RYA Introduction to Navigation	Melanie Bartlett	G77
RYA ICC Handbook	Rob Gibson	G81
RYA Day Skipper Handbook Motor	Jon Mendez	G97
RYA Inland Waterways Handbook	Andy Newman	G102
RYA Boat Safety Handbook	Keith Colwell	E-G103
RYA Advanced Powerboat Handbook	Paul Glatzel	G108
RYA Weather Handbook	Chris Tibbs	G133
RYA Training Almanac (Northern Hemisphere)	RYA	TAN
RYA Training Almanac (Southern Hemisphere)	RYA	TAS
RYA Practice Charts (Northern Hemisphere)	RYA	TC3/TC4
RYA Practice Charts (Southern Hemisphere)	RYA	TC5/TC6
RYA Yachtmaster Shorebased Notes	RYA	YSN

Appendix 4 – Powerboating and the Environment

Boating in all its forms, not just under power, has the potential to impact on the marine environment. There is both national and international legislation that exists to ensure that the marine environment is protected and substantial penalties apply for breach of these laws. As Instructors you are well placed to ensure new participants are aware of this and able to ensure we continue to enjoy freedom on the water.

Comprehensive information on both the legal and practical aspects, including products available, can be found at **www.rya.org.uk/knowledge/environment** and The Green Blue website at **www.thegreenblue.org.uk**. Here are a just a few tips that you can incorporate into your training.

Refuelling and Discharging your Bilge Water

Discharge of oil or oily wastes into the water is an offence. Oils can enter the water during everyday operations such as refuelling and pumping the bilge. Spill kits suitable for small craft are available and can easily be carried on board. As routine practice it is good to have oil absorbent 'socks' in the bilge to mop up any oil that finds its way there. Safety-fill nozzles are also available for refuelling from portable tanks. If you do spill oil or fuel into the water, never use detergents as this only adds to the pollutants.

Waste on Board

Dumping waste at sea, even food waste within three miles of shore, is an offence. Ideally, leave any excess packaging ashore before you leave for the day but secure all rubbish on board and ensure nothing blows over the side. If it does, practise your man-overboard skills! Use recycling facilities ashore where available, and have a couple of separate bags onboard to store your waste.

Cleaning

Washing down the boat at the end of the day can often be achieved by a little extra elbow grease. If detergents are used, choose more environmentally sensitive ones and avoid those that contain chlorine, phosphates or bleach. This also applies to detergents used in sinks and toilets on board. Take care to wash off trailers and hulls, particularly when transporting boats, as species can hitch-hike and cause major problems when they colonise a new area.

Speed, Wash and Disturbance

Coastal and inland waterways play host to rich wildlife, and many habitats and species are protected by law. Boat users enjoy freedom on the water; however, with freedom comes responsibility. If you come across wildlife while afloat, take care not to harass or damage it. Disturbance can affect feeding and breeding regimes. Think about your speed and the wash created when you are close to the shore to avoid erosion of habitats and disturbing feeding and nesting sites. Use recognised landing places when you go ashore.

Toilets on Board

International laws regulate the use of sea toilets. Use shorebased facilities wherever possible and never open sea toilets in marinas, rivers and low tidal flushing areas.

Index

A

Admiralty Charts, Symbols and Abbreviations Used on	93
adrift, being	76
Advanced Powerboat Day & Night Course, RYA	94–109
aim	94
boat handling	94–98
boat control in waves	95
downwind driving	96
hull forms, characteristics of	96
killcords	98
knowledge required	94
man overboard	98
tide, effects of	98
trim	97
turning in confined space	98
upwind driving	95
wind, effects of	98
considerations, practical	94
emergency situations	103–104
engines, use of	102–103
checks to be made	102–103
knowledge required	102
examiners, notes for	105–109
exam	105–109
authorisation	105
barriers	109
boat and venue	106
candidate numbers	107
conduct	107
duration	107
eligibility	106
fee	105
partial re-examination	109
pass/fail decision	108
post-exam debrief	108
report	109
scenarios	107
stress management	107–108
IRPCS	101
meteorology	101
night cruising	105
passage making	99
pilotage	100
preparation for sea	94
responsibilities as skipper	99
rules of the road	101
syllabus	94
theory	101
anchor, recovery of	71–72
approach	72
escape	72
knowledge required	72
manoeuvre	72
planning	71
theory	72
anchoring	70–71, 72
aim	70
approach	71
escape	71
inland waterways	140
knowledge required	72
manoeuvre	71
personal watercraft	124
preparation	70
success indicator	70
theory	72
assessment of students' abilities	32
awareness of other water users	76, 78

B

'bank effect' (interaction)	130
barges	127, 129, 130, 139
	see also Inland Waterways Scheme, RYA
batteries, siting of	75
bearing and distance	93
bearings, back	100
bearings, true and magnetic	92
boat control in waves and rough water	78, 95
boat handling theory	78–79
knowledge required	78
boat preparation	45–46, 94
boat registration schemes	75
boats, displacement, handling characteristics	78
briefing	28–31
debrief	29–31
feedback methods, common elements	30
'hamburger' ('sandwich' or 'layer cake') feedback model	30
'traffic light' feedback model	31

points to include   29
task   29
buoyage systems   77, 126
  lateral and cardinal   93
buoyancy aids   46, 123 see also
                                            lifejackets
bylaws, local   75, 125

C

canal cruising   see Inland Waterways
                                        Scheme, RYA
capsized personal watercraft, righting   125
carbon monoxide   10
care, duty of   9
CE mark   78
certificates   33, 38, 128–129
chart plotters   75, 84, 92, 99
chart symbols   77, 93
charts   77
  laminated   93
  personal watercraft   126
Charts, Admiralty, Symbols and   93
Abbreviations Used on
clearing lines   100
coaching, techniques for   see instructing,
                                      techniques for
coaching processes   12
coaching skills   11, 12
Coastguard   75, 103, 104
cold shock   69, 86, 104, 140
collision avoidance on inland   141
waterways
collisions, preventing   see IRPCS
coming alongside another craft,   116
pontoon or floating dock
(personal watercraft)
coming alongside on inland waterways
  single-handed   132
  using crew   131
coming alongside jetty or pontoon   53–64
  aim   53
  downtide approach   57–59
    approach   57
    escape   58
    manoeuvre   57
    planning   57
  method, determining   53
  success indicator   53
  tide flowing away from   63–64
  pontoon face
    approach   63

escape   64
manoeuvre   63
planning   63
tide flowing onto pontoon face   60
tide running parallel to   54–55, 56
chosen face
  approach   54
  escape   55
  manoeuvre   54–55
  planning   54
  theory   56
communication skills   19–20
  communicating while afloat   20
  communication blocks   19
  effective communication   20
  non-verbal messages   19
  ways of communicating   19
communication with other craft   76
compass, use of   77
compass bearings   93
conduct, code of   5
considerations, general   9
controls, effect of   79
cornering at   see planing speeds,
planing speeds   control and cornering
                              at (personal watercraft)
course to steer, plotting   92
courtesy to others   124
craft, types of   75
crew, alerting   45
crew members and their welfare   78, 95, 99
crew position   45
current, effect on craft   79

D

disabled craft   76
discrimination   6
distress calls, issuing   76, 92, 103, 104
distress signals   76, 104
downwind driving   96

E

EDICTS powerboat   11–12, 113, 127
teaching model
electrical checks   103
electrical wiring, siting of   75
emergency action   76
emergency situations   103–104
  personal watercraft   122, 125
engine checks   75, 94, 102–103, 140

engine maintenance and fault diagnosis ... 75, 140

engine spares ... 103

engine tell-tale check ... 44

engine trim ... 79

engines, outboard ... 75, 79

engines and drives, types of ... 75

environment, care of (inland waterways) ... 127 *see also Appendix 4*

equality policy ... 6

ethics, code of ... 5

F

fear, overcoming ... 17, 21

fire extinguishers ... 75, 76

fire precautions ... 76, 103

fires, fighting ... 76, 103

flares ... 81, 104

fuel system checks ... 94, 103

fuel tanks and lines, siting of ... 75

G

gear, securing and stowing ... 94

GPS (global position system) ... 75, 80, 92, 93

H

health declarations ... 9

helicopter rescue procedures ... 104

helm, changing ... 45

holding off ... 50

hull damage ... 76, 103

hulls, different, advantages and disadvantages ... 75, 96

hypothermia ... 104

I

information, absorbing ... 13

Inland Waterways Scheme, RYA ... 127–141

   anchoring ... 140

   coming alongside – single-handed ... 132

   coming alongside – using crew ... 131

   considerations ... 129–130

   Inland Waterways Instructor course ... 127–129

      certificates ... 128–129

      moderation ... 128–129

      syllabus ... 127

   leaving bank – single-handed ... 134

      by 'springing-off' ... 134–135

leaving bank – using crew ... 133

locks, using ... 136–137

   aim ... 136

   approach ... 137

   considerations ... 136–137

   escape ... 137

   man overboard ... 139

   manoeuvre ... 137

   planning ... 137

   success indicator ... 136

man overboard ... 138–139

   locks ... 139

   narrow canals and waterways ... 138

   preventative measures ... 138

   success indicator ... 138

   wider rivers and estuaries ... 139

theory ... 140–141

   boat handling ... 141

   boat safety ... 141

   bridges ... 141

   collision avoidance ... 141

   deckwork ... 140

   engines ... 140

   environment, care of ... 141

   helming ... 141

   locks ... 141

   personal safety ... 140

   tunnels ... 141

turning using winding hole ... 135

instructing, techniques for ... 11–32

   briefing ... *see briefing*

   certificates ... 33

   coaching processes ... 12

   coaching skills ... 11, 12

   communication skills ... *see communication skills*

   debriefing ... *see briefing: debrief*

   EDICTS powerboat teaching model ... 11–12, 113, 127

   fear, overcoming ... 17

   feedback ... *see briefing: debrief*

   information, absorbing ... 13

   instructing skills ... 11, 12

   instructor, students' perception of ... 18, 22

   learners, types of ... 13

   learning, barriers to ... 17

   learning, four stages of ... 14–15

   learning, tips for reinforcing ... 14

   learning motivation ... 16

   learning process ... 16

learning through doing   12–13
people skills for instructors   18
presentation skills   see presentation
                                        skills
presentations, structuring   22–23
questions, handling   24–25
students, what needs to be   18
known about
students' abilities, assessing   32
students' perception of instructor 18, 22
visual aids, use of   see visual aids,
                                     use of
  instructing skills   11, 12
instructor, students' perception of   18, 22
instructor health declaration   9
instructor position   45
instruments, plotting   92
insurance   75
interaction ('bank effect')   130
IRPCS (International   65, 76, 77, 83,
Regulations for Preventing   93, 101, 118
Collisions at Sea)
  personal watercraft   118, 120
  sound signals   125

J

jetty, coming alongside   see coming
                              alongside jetty
                                  or pontoon
jetty, leaving   see leaving jetty
                                  or pontoon

K

killcords   44, 81, 82, 98, 114

L

latitude   92
launching   46–48
  aim   46
  approach   47
  escape   48
  knowledge required   48
  manoeuvre   48
  personal watercraft   124
  preparation   47
  success indicator   46
  theory   48
leading lines   100
learners, types of   13
learning, barriers to   17

learning, four stages of   14–15
learning, tips for reinforcing   14
learning model,   34, 113, 127
PAME powerboat
learning motivation   16
learning process   16
learning through doing   12–13
leaving bank (inland waterways)
  single-handed   134
    by 'springing-off'   134–135
  using crew   133
leaving jetty or pontoon   55–56
  downtide – strong tide   59
  downtide – weak tide   58
  personal watercraft   117
  tide flowing away from pontoon face   64
  tide flowing onto pontoon face –   62
  strong tide
  tide flowing onto pontoon face –   61
  weak tide
  tide running parallel to   55–56
  chosen face
    light tide   55
    preparation   55
    strong tide   56
    theory   56
lee shores   124
lifejackets   9, 46, 81, 82, 130, 140 see also
                              buoyancy aids
loading of boat, effect of   78
locks, using   136–137
  aim   136
  approach   137
  considerations   136–137
  escape   137
  man overboard   139
  manoeuvre   137
  marina   92
  planning   137
  success indicator   136–137
  theory   137
longitude   92
lookout, keeping   105

M

maintenance, personal watercraft   126
maintenance checks, periodic 75, 103, 140
man overboard (MOB)   66–69, 98
  aim   66
  downwind (drift) method   68–69

approach 68
escape 69
manoeuvre 68
preparation 68
inland waterways 138–139
locks 139
narrow canals and waterways 138
preventative measures 138
success indicator 138
wider rivers and estuaries 139
knowledge required 69
personal watercraft 117–118
approach 117
escape 117
manoeuvre 117
preparation 117
prevention 66, 138
success indicator 66, 138
theory 69
upwind method 66–67
approach 67
escape 67
manoeuvre 67
preparation 66
manoeuvres, *see* planing-speed
planing-speed manoeuvres
marina locks, use of 92
yacht deck qualifications 87
'Mayday' calls 76, 92, 103, 104
medical conditions 9
medical emergencies 103
meteorology 101 *see also*
weather forecasts
mooring, leaving 52–53
approach 52
escape 53
manoeuvre 53
preparation 52
theory 53
mooring, picking up 51–52
aim 51
approach 51
escape 52
manoeuvre 52
preparation 51
success indicator 51

N

narrowboats 127, 129, 130, 139 *see also*
Inland Waterways Scheme, RYA

navigation 92–93
electronic 93, 99 *see also*
chart plotters; GPS
at higher speed 99
personal watercraft 126
night cruising 105

O

Officer of the Watch (OOW) 85, 87, 88
training record book 87–88
'one hand gear, one hand steer' rule 45
outboard engines 75, 79
own-boat tuition 8

P

PAME powerboat 34, 113, 127
learning model,
'Pan Pan' calls 103
passage planning 77, 93, 99
people skills for instructors 18
personal watercraft (PW)
checks, pre-launch and 123
pre-departure
equipment, essential 123
handling 114
layout of 123
types of 122
Personal Watercraft Scheme, RYA 110–126
aftercare 126
anchoring 124
boarding and starting 124
from deep water 122
capsized PW, righting 125
checks, pre-launch and 123
pre-departure
collision avoidance 118, 125
coming alongside another craft, 116
pontoon or floating dock
considerations, practical 113
courtesy to others 124
drysuits 123
EDICTS teaching model 113
emergencies 122, 125
equipment, essential 123
familiarisation 124
hand signals 113
IRPCS 118, 125
launching 124
leaving from alongside a pontoon 117
lee shores 124

maintenance 126
man overboard *see* man overboard: personal watercraft
navigation 126
PAME student model 113
personal buoyancy 123
personal watercraft, layout of 123
personal watercraft handling 114
Personal Watercraft Instructor Course 110–112
    moderation 112
    syllabus 111
planing speeds, control and cornering at *see* planing speeds, control and cornering (personal watercraft)
recovery 124, 126
'rules of the road' 118–119, 125
safety 123, 124
slow speed, controlling at 114
syllabus 112–113
theory 122–123
    knowledge required 122
trim 124
weather 124
wetsuits 123
pilot books 93
pilotage 77, 93, 100
planning-speed manoeuvres 73–74, 79
    aim 73
    approach 73
    escape 74
    manoeuvre 73
    preparation 73
    slowing down 74
    success indicator 73
    trim 74, 79
    turning at high speed 73–74
planing speeds, control and cornering at (personal watercraft) 120–121
    aim 120
    acceleration 121
    box course 120
    deceleration 121
    escape 120
    first planning-speed ride 120
    fast straights, fast corners 121
    fast straights, slow corners 121
    fast straights, wide corners 121
    manoeuvre 120
    plan 120

slalom exercise 121
tasks 121
plotting course to steer 92
pontoon, coming alongside *see* coming alongside jetty or pontoon
pontoon, leaving *see* leaving jetty or pontoon
powerboat, types of 75
Powerboat Level 2 – Powerboat handling course, RYA 44–79
    anchor, recovery of *see* anchor, recovery of
    anchoring *see* anchoring
    boat preparation 45–46
    coming alongside jetty or pontoon *see* coming alongside jetty or pontoon
    holding off 50
    instructing, golden rules for 44–45
    killcords 44
    launching *see* launching
    leaving mooring *see* mooring, leaving
    man overboard *see* man overboard
    manoeuvres, planing-speed *see* planing-speed manoeuvres
    mooring, picking up *see* mooring, picking up
    recovery 48
    slow speed familiarisation 49
    specifications 44
    theory 75–79 *see also* individual subheadings
        boat handling *see* boat handling theory
        knowledge required 75
turning in confined space 65, 98
preparation of powerboat for sea 45–46, 94
presentation skills 21–22
    appearance 22, 24
    body movements 22, 24
    content 21
    fear of presenting 21
    how words said 22
    words used 21
presentations, structuring 22–23
'propwalk' 129–130, 135
propeller angle on planing boats, effects of 79
propeller check 44
propellers, changing, and characteristics of 102

propulsion, alternative means of 76

Q

questions, handling 24–25

R

radar 99
Recognised Training Centres (RTCs) 7–8
   administration 8
   advertising 8
   categories 7
   lifejackets policy 130
   own-boat tuition 8
   recognition, gaining 7
   recognition conditions 8
recovery, personal watercraft 124, 126
recovery, powerboat 48
regulations, local 75
rescue procedures, helicopter 104
responsibilities 76
responsibilities as skipper 99
'reverse bank effect' 130
'rules of the road' see IRPCS
RYA (Royal Yachting Association)
   certificates 33, 38, 128–129
   code of ethics and conduct 5
   courses see RYA courses
   equality policy 6–7
   Inland Waterways see Inland Waterways
   Scheme Scheme, RYA
   Instructor awards 10
   logo 8
   name 8
   organisation 7–8
   Personal Watercraft see Personal
   Scheme Watercraft
    Scheme, RYA
   Power Schemes instructor log 139
   Powerboat Instructor conversions 41–42
      Powerboat Instructor to 41
      Personal Watercraft Instructor
      RYA Yachtmaster Instructor to 42
      Powerboat Instructor
   Powerboat Scheme and structure 43
   Powerboat Trainer 40
   pre-instructor skills assessment 138
   RYA courses
   Advanced Powerboat see Advanced
   Day & Night Powerboat Day &
    Night Course, RYA

Advanced Powerboat 38–40
Instructor Course
   prerequisites 39
   syllabus 39–40
Inland Waterways Instructor 127–129
   certificates 128–129
   moderation 128–129
   syllabus 127
Intermediate Powerboat 90–93
Day Cruising Course
   aim 90
   knowledge required 92
   skills taught 90–91
   syllabus 90
   theory 91–93
   trimming for rougher conditions 91
Personal Watercraft 110–112
Instructor Course
   moderation 112
   syllabus 111
Powerboat Instructor Course 35–38
   certificate validity 38
   moderation 38
   pre-entry skills assessment 35, 36
   prerequisites 36
   specifications 35
   syllabus 37
Powerboat Level 1 – 45
Start powerboating
Powerboat Level 2 – see Powerboat
Powerboat handling Level 2 –
    Powerboat
Tender Operator Course 80–89
   aim 80
   theory 87–89
handling course, RYA
   Powerboat Trainer 40
   Safety Boat Course 40–41

S

safety, inland waterways 138, 140, 141
safety, personal watercraft 123, 124
search patterns 104
seating, adequate 78, 95
seating arrangements 75
shipping forecasts 101 see also
    weather forecasts
shock, cold 69, 104, 140
sinking, action to prevent 76, 103
slow speed familiarisation 49

slowing down 74, 117–118
sound signals 125
soundings 100
STCW95 88
steering with outboard engines 79
stopping distances 114–115
student health declaration 9
students, what needs to be known about 18
students' abilities, assessing 32
students' perception of instructor 18, 22
students' powerboat 34, 113, 127
learning model, PAME
swimmers 9
synoptic charts 101 *see also* weather forecasts

T

task structure 34
teaching model, 11–12, 113, 127
EDICTS powerboat
Tender Operator Course, RYA 80–89
    boat handling 82
    documents 88
    emergency situations 86
    life saving apparatus (LSA) 81, 82, 83, 84
    navigation equipment 80
    pilotage
        day 84–85
        night 85–86
    preparation 80
    procedures, pre-departure 81
    rules of the road 83
    safety 83–84
    theory 87–89
tidal diamonds 93
tidal heights 92, 126
tidal streams 77, 93, 98, 126
    effect on craft 79
tide tables 126
tides 77, 126
    effects of 98
towed, being 103
    personal watercraft 122
towing 76, 103
    personal watercraft 122
towlines, personal watercraft 122
Training Centres, *see* Recognised
Recognised Training Centres (RTCs)
transits 98, 100
    on inland waterways 131, 132, 140

trim, personal watercraft 124
trimming powerboat 74, 79, 91, 97
turning in confined space 65, 98
turning at high speed 73–74
turning using winding hole 135
(inland waterways)
twin-engine vessels 94

U

upwind driving 95

V

VHF DSC 104
visibility, restricted 76
visual aids, use of 25–28
    accessibility 27–28
        dyslexic people 2, 28
        flip chart use 28
        font style 27
        paper 27
        presentation style 27
        writing style 28
    blackboards 25
    data projectors 26
    DVDs 26
    flip charts 26, 28
    models 26
    'real thing' 26
    tips, general 25, 27
    white boards 25

W

wash, effects of 78
waypoints 93
weather forecasts 101 *see also* meteorology
    information sources and 75, 92
    interpretation
    personal watercraft 124
wind, effects of 98
winding holes 135
'windlass' handles 137
winds, cross 130
wiring, siting of 75